SAND
AND
BLOOD

Bold Type Books
116 East 16th Street, 8th Floor New York, NY 10003
www.boldtypebooks.org
@BoldTypeBooks

Printed in the United States of America

First Edition: June 2019

Published by Bold Type Books, an imprint of Perseus Books, LLC, a subsidiary of Hachette Book Group, Inc. Bold Type Books is a co-publishing venture of the Type Media Center and Perseus Books.

The Hachette Speakers Bureau provides a wide range of authors for speaking events. To find out more, go to www.hachettespeakersbureau.com or call (866) 376-6591.

The publisher is not responsible for websites (or their content) that are not owned by the publisher.

A portion of Chapter 5 originally appeared in the *Texas Observer* ("Graves of Shame," 2015) and appears here courtesy of *Texas Observer*.

A section from Chapter 6 originally appeared in Salon.com ("Cruelty on the Border," 2012) and appears here courtesy of Salon.

Print book interior design by Amnet Systems.

Library of Congress Control Number: 2019937320

ISBN: 978-1-56858-847-6 (hardcover)
ISBN: 978-1-56858-846-9 (e-book)

LSC-C

10 9 8 7 6 5 4 3 2 1

JOHN CARLOS FREY

SAND AND BLOOD

AMERICA'S STEALTH WAR

on the MEXICO BORDER

BOLD TYPE
BOOKS
NEW YORK

To my mother, an immigrant from Mexico who came to America to provide a better life for me and my siblings, and to all the mothers and fathers who had the same intention and lost their lives in the attempt.

Contents

Introduction

I was born in Tijuana, Mexico, and my family moved to the United States in 1965 when I was a toddler. Even though I was born in a foreign country, I am a US citizen because my father was. It took me a long time to realize that by this simple twist of fate—the fact that my parent was a citizen—my circumstances were radically different from those of most people born in Mexico, affording me benefits that my counterparts could not access.

In the United States, we lived in a rural part of southern San Diego, California. From my family home, I could see Tijuana just a few hundred yards to the south. The phenomenon of migration was something I witnessed every day. Migrants seeking work in the United States would cross the border and quickly make their way northward, running through our backyard at night on their journey. US Border Patrol agents usually chased them. A Border Patrol helicopter would fly over every night; sometimes, its spotlight would cross my bedroom window, making the whole room as bright as day.

Occasionally the neighborhood kids would play in nearby open fields, trying to run into the helicopter spotlight. When we got close to it, we would stir up dirt, creating a noticeable cloud of dust and making it seem like a migrant group had just run through the area. Sometimes, the helicopter spotlight would linger on the cloud we had created, and we would all hide under bushes, scared but giggling. Eventually, we would get spooked and run to the safety of our homes. We never sensed that we were in any real danger. Looking back, I realize that it was not a great idea to taunt federal law enforcement officials, but at the time, it was normal for us. It's what we did for fun. Didn't every kid play migrant on the run? Didn't every kid grow up this way?

I was never taught to fear the migrants, either. My parents told me that they were mostly poor people coming to California to work on the farms or on construction sites. Sometimes, on my walk to school, I would see migrants lying under cars to stay out of the damp weather. They were usually young men in their twenties and thirties; I rarely saw women or families. Sometimes I would wave or talk to them and continue on my way. At the time, there was no real border fence separating San Diego from Tijuana. Marking the borderline was a remnant of a chain-link fence that had been smashed and destroyed years prior. It was no barrier or deterrent. You could just tell that this was where one country started and the other ended. People would gather along the line and picnic or play soccer and music. It was a kind of no-man's-land.

Hundreds of migrants would gather along this strange strip of land every night. They would wait for a moment when the helicopter and Border Patrol vehicles were far enough away, and small groups would run together across the border, knowing that guards would not be able to catch them all. As a Border Patrol vehicle approached, the migrants would scatter, hide in the brush, or keep running. If a migrant could avoid the Border Patrol for a few miles, he was usually safe in the United States.

This game of cat and mouse wasn't particularly effective from the perspective of the Border Patrol. I heard at the time that for every two migrants who were caught, more than ten would get across. That seemed about right, because a Border Patrol vehicle could only hold a few, and migrants usually came in large groups—too big for the patrols to manage.

It wasn't long before the Border Patrol presence touched our lives more directly. One day when I was about twelve, I went for a walk with my mother down by the nearby open fields and farms. It was winter and the rainy season, which always brings a springlike bloom of plants and flowers. My mom loved to see the flowers, and I liked to play in the seasonal stream that was full of tadpoles. As we left the neighborhood and walked near the Tijuana River, I ran ahead of my mother to see what I could find in the water below. I made this trek frequently, sometimes with her and many times alone. It was my favorite place to explore. I could see Mexico in front of me and even hear sounds of traffic and music coming from the nearby city of Tijuana, just several hundred yards away.

My mother was a Mexican woman with dark features and dark skin. She spoke English with a thick Mexican accent. That day, as she walked seemingly alone along the road near the US-Mexico border, moving toward where I was, she caught the attention of a Border Patrol agent who was looking for migrants. Agents would drive up and down our neighborhood streets regularly, always on the lookout for brown faces. This one stopped to question my mother about her immigration status, asking for identification. She told him she lived just up the road and could get her ID from home. The agent didn't believe her. She told him that her husband was in the house and that he could stop by and ask him. He still did not believe her. She told him she had lived in the United States for twenty years and that I, her son, was playing nearby. Instead of listening to my mother's pleas, the agent put her in handcuffs and then in the back of his patrol car. He took her to the Imperial Beach Border Patrol station, where she was processed and held in a cell. Within a few hours, she had been deported to Tijuana.

A few minutes after she had been taken away, I came back from the river's edge to find my mother missing. I called for her and walked up and down the road but found no trace of her. I ran home and told my father. He quickly called the police, and we all waited. We suspected that the Border Patrol had taken her, but since I hadn't seen anything, we weren't sure. For more than twenty-four hours, we knew nothing about what had happened to her.

Later the next day, after she had arrived in Tijuana, she contacted us to let us know where she was. We felt relieved that she was safe but also angry that she had been deported because of the color of her skin—she was, after all, a legal US resident. My father left immediately to bring her green card so she could get back home. She never went for that walk again, and she never left the house without carrying her green card and driver's license.

- - -

I never forgot that moment. There were many others that made me question US policy at the border. Before I became an investigative reporter, I noticed how the landscape changed near my childhood home. I saw more agents patrolling my neighborhood. There always seemed to be a helicopter in the air, especially at night. The border fence was rising—haphazardly at first—then walls followed years later. The area grew more militarized by the year.

This was all during the late 1970s. Border security was a part of growing up so close to Mexico, but it was clear that more migrants crossed the border illegally than were caught. The United States needed farmworkers, construction labor, maids, and busboys. The US government put up a thin line of defense that allowed the "cheap" labor in while demonstrating some attempt at stopping the constant flow of migrants. It appeared that border security at the time was just a show for the public. Some migrants were caught, but not enough to hurt the US businesses that relied on the steady stream of labor. The pull into the United States from Mexico was stronger than the defense against it. It wasn't until the 1980s that security strategy changed—and mostly for political reasons.

What was once a weak show of force and anemic attempt to stop illegal immigration became a more heavy-handed and militaristic approach to catch migrants. A warlike stance began to take shape against a population that was poor and mostly unarmed. Politicians pulled the levers and commanded the troops. Defense contractors escalated the tensions while companies in need of masses of laborers tried to tamp them down. Migrants were caught in the middle.

Every time I returned to visit family in southern San Diego, I noticed more border guards, more border fencing, more helicopters. It was getting serious. "Playing army" with the Border Patrol helicopter would now be a life-and-death exercise. It bothered me that the pristine natural surroundings I had grown up in had been permanently scarred to keep poor people from entering the United States—people who were coming to work. It made little sense to me. It was clear that we needed the cheap labor, and we exploited it—yet we were willing to spend billions to make a show of force against the workers we were employing.

My last fifteen years as a journalist along the border have revealed much pain and more inept and ineffective policy, with few of its intended positive results. Border security has never been stronger—we have never had so many guards and so many walls; we have never spent so many billions of dollars. Yet migrants with little in terms of resources, power, or skill still get across, and businesses in the United States still rely on their labor. The country still has a need for "cheap labor"; men, women, and children from Mexico—and farther south—still need work and safety from dangers in their home countries. The latter issues have not been addressed, so the migration continues—except now, it has a terrible human price. We are witnessing the effects of war and the inhumane policies of deterrence at all costs along the southern border. People are disappearing, and people are dying. Thousands have perished, and it is likely that thousands more will, well into the future.

In these pages, using my experience, reporting, and knowledge, I seek to prove a point. We are using the tactics and the machinery of war against all who dare to cross the US-Mexico border. US military might meets them with all its consequences and lack of compassion or responsibility. In war there are few rules and many casualties. Although the United States has not formally declared war on these targets, the results of our policies at the border sure look a lot like the effects of war, with a mounting death toll and no one held to account. We are not addressing the root causes of migration—and until we do, we will never be able to manage the flow of humanity. We are using a militaristic approach against an enemy that does not exist. As long as the push to fortify the border continues, as seems likely—no politician has yet challenged the assumed need for border security—the human costs will continue to accumulate.

As I write this, I am watching history unfold at the US-Mexico border as I have never seen it before. Trump has taken on the mantle of border security more aggressively and less thoughtfully than any president before him, and it is clear that past administrations have laid an ample number of tools at his feet to allow him to create great chaos and destruction. I noted that I've been reporting about the border for the past fifteen years. Politicians' xenophobic rhetoric used to be somewhat nuanced, but no longer. That we could achieve comprehensive immigration reform or a sober approach to migration and all its complexities now seems impossible.

It's worse than ever before, and migrants are suffering need-lessly. But the groundwork was laid long before Trump. Year after year, the US-Mexico border has become increasingly mili-tarized and with far too little public acknowledgment. The Bor-der Patrol's policing force keeps growing, and no one is asking if the zeal to seal the border is having a positive or negative effect. Is US border policy effective at keeping migrants in their home countries? Shouldn't that be the metric by which we measure it? If it is, border policy has failed. Defense contractors have had a field day, descending like vultures picking at the scraps Congress throws them with every new administration. And yet too many of their supposedly innovative approaches have back-fired. Migrants have died by the thousands, and still people keep coming. Now we've handed this massive infrastructure over to Trump with his promise that he will do more of the same, and the effects, as we're coming to realize, will be even more devastating.

If you live along the border, where nearly eight million Americans make their homes, you know that it's different from any other part of the United States. The Spanish language and the Mexican culture are everywhere. It is difficult to differenti-ate US and Mexican traditions; the two have melded. In places along the US side of the border, it is difficult to even distinguish which side of the border you're on. It can feel like you're in Mexico, because the Latino influence is so strong—after all, it *was* Mexico over 150 years ago. But that's not all that makes it unique. It can seem like a war zone. Border Patrol agents in trucks, Humvees, jeeps, and helicopters are part of the land-scape. You can see arrests of migrants on any given day, even on a busy road. There are checkpoints on every major highway heading north from Mexico, and everyone has to stop at each one. And if you get close to Mexico itself, there are walls, fenc-ing, and barriers already existing along seven hundred miles of the border. In many port towns—such as San Diego, El Paso, Nogales, Laredo, and Brownsville—the wall is a constant backdrop. In some places, the wall is formidable, like in San Diego; in other towns, it simply scars the landscape. The closer you get to the border, the more militarized it becomes. Camera arrays sit atop walls. Customs agents, border agents, and ICE agents are everywhere—all to stop migrants.

The effects of militarization do not end at the border. The creation of ICE has stretched the immigration police presence into all areas of the interior of the United States. ICE conducts raids in workplaces and outside of courthouses, dressed under-cover and driving unmarked vehicles. It is a clandestine police force looking for immigrants who may have committed crimes or overstayed their visas. The hunt for immigrants is now every-where. In the past fifteen years, prisons have sprung up in every state to house all the immigrants that need to be processed—it has become a big business. The United States has become the largest jailer of immigrants in the world, most of whom have committed no criminal offenses other than possible immigra-tion violations—and most of whom are housed in private, for-profit detention facilities.

US policy at the border also seems to have bypassed the Constitution. It is a zone where inspections can happen to any-one without probable cause and use of force can go unchecked without repercussion. Immigrants both legal and undocu-mented have been stripped of civil liberties, and the violations continue—to the point of the removal of children from their parents or even death.

The war against migrants costs in the tens of billions of dollars annually. This is a rough estimate including the annual budgets for ICE, customs agents, and Border Patrol as well as infrastruc-ture projects, but it does not take into account the cost of lost family income due to deportation or the cost of thousands of lives lost. The taxpayer cost is high. Most of the dollars are spent on border security, with no real metric to determine its efficacy.

In the rush to increase border security, the United States seems to have ignored the fact that most migrants are desperate and will try anything to save themselves and their families. We have yet to apply reason or measure to this reality of migration. If you create a scenario where people may die in the attempt to cross into the United States, if they have run out of all other options, they will attempt it anyway. If you build a wall, they will scale it or tunnel under it or cut a hole through it. If you incarcerate people, their families will come anyway. If you separate a mother from her child, she will come anyway. Weapons, walls, and more border guards do not put food on the table for a Central American family who, facing drought and famine or gang violence in its own country, has decided to risk its members' lives to cross the border.

For more than thirty years, the United States has engaged in a militaristic approach to solve the complex issues of migration, and it hasn't worked. My hope is that this book can shed light on the mistreatment of immigrants and the injustice perpetrated by US policy so that we may find a path forward that does justice to the immigrant spirit of America.

1

Seeds of War

Since its inception in 1924, the U.S. Border Patrol has had a proud history of service to our nation. Although enormous changes have affected nearly every aspect of its operations from its earliest days, the basic values that helped shape the Patrol in the early years; professionalism, honor, integrity, respect for human life, and a shared effort, have remained.

—*From the official website of the US Department of Homeland Security*

Anti-immigrant sentiments in the United States can be traced back to even before the founding of the country. Benjamin Franklin said in 1753 of a German immigrant wave, "Those who come hither are generally of the most ignorant stupid sort of their own nation . . . they come in droves. They will soon so outnumber us, that all the advantages we have will not in my opinion be able to preserve our language, and even our government will become precarious."[1] Current leaders could have spoken those words today, and they underscore the scapegoating of immigrants as part of US history. Strong rhetoric vilifying immigrants is harmful, and today there appears to be an all-out war against them. The United States has engaged in policy and procedure that involves military-style tactics to deter migration and has amassed a casualty list of injured and deceased that numbers in the tens of thousands.

The war on migrants entering the United States has deep roots, stemming from policies that date back to the 1880s. Since then, each administration and congress has built upon the last to expand this war, but in just the last few decades, it has accelerated at an unprecedented pace. Politicians using fear to win votes have made the threat of invasion from immigrants sound real, even if it is unfounded, and defense contractors looking for new places to sell their equipment have used it as well.

The Border Patrol wasn't formally established until 1924, but there were federal government patrols of the American Southwest border as early as 1904.[2] According to the official history of US Customs and Border Protection (CBP), the US military patrolled the border then, looking for and apprehending mostly Chinese immigrants. Chinese immigrant laborers had worked in California's gold rush by the thousands, but when these immigrants began to settle in neighborhoods and create their own communities, especially in California, racial divides began to appear. The Chinese Exclusion Act of 1882, which prohibited Chinese laborers from emigrating to the United States, passed in response to the wave of Chinese immigrants arriving to work. One of the border guards' first tasks was to make sure that such immigrants were not sneaking across the US-Mexico border.

Even before the formation of the US Border Patrol, military tactics had kept immigrants from entering the country as early as 1904. Although only a handful of horseback-riding inspectors from the office of US Immigration Service, referred to as Mounted Guards, did most of the sparse patrolling of the US-Mexico border—never totaling more than seventy-five men—military troops performed intermittent border patrolling

between El Paso and California[3] when needed. Military personnel also trained federal agents in military-style tactics in the early
days. Although military personnel could not arrest immigrants,
they directed them to immigration inspection stations, where
they would be processed and deported. Most migrants, unless
caught in the commission of a crime, would just be sent back
across the border to Mexico directly after being apprehended.

Immigration laws were already restrictive prior to the formation of the Border Patrol, and a nationalistic streak ran through
much of the legislation. Not only were Chinese immigrants
restricted from coming to the United States, but by the time
the first Border Patrol agent was formally installed, US law had
restricted immigration to all "Asians, illiterates, prostitutes,
criminals, contract laborers, unaccompanied children, idiots,
epileptics, the insane, the diseased and defective, alcoholics,
beggars, polygamists, anarchists," and more.[4] Nationalists lob-
bied to add more nationalities to the list of restricted sources of
immigration, including Mexican, but agricultural lobbyists in
Texas and California fought to keep restrictions off the necessary labor pool that they relied on.

In the early 1900s, no one considered the border a lawless or
dangerous place. There was illegal immigration; an underground
smuggling trade for Asian workers had been established, along
with the importation of some forbidden vices such as booze and
prostitutes. As early as the formation of the Border Patrol, the
undesirable and restricted immigrants were commonly referred
to as "the enemy."[5]

Mexican migrants crossed the border regularly, if not daily,
for work on the farms in the booming agricultural regions of
California, Texas, and Arizona. Many lived in border towns and
worked in the United States, returning to their homes in Mexico
each night. Others sought employment on railroad construction
jobs. Most Mexican migrants who wanted to work in the United
States could do so without facing any legal hurdles. But that
would soon change.

There were fears among white lawmakers in Washington, DC, that Mexican culture and deep poverty would take hold in America, degrading its fabric and culture. In 1924, Congressman John C. Box of Texas expressed the sentiments of other politicians who believed in immigration restriction: "The continuance of a desirable character of citizenship is the fundamental purpose of our immigration laws. Incidental to this are the avoidance of social and racial problems, the upholding of American standards of wages and living and the maintenance of order. All of these purposes will be violated by increasing the Mexican population of the country."[6] The pressure to keep immigrants out has, from its earliest days, been linked to racist sentiments.

Border security intensified in the 1920s, first in the wake of the ratification of the Eighteenth Amendment in 1920, which banned the manufacture, sale, and transportation of alcohol. The amendment emphasized the protection of the southern and northern borders as well as seaports. Prohibition brought the need for border security to the forefront of lawmakers' actions. Illegal immigration was not as strong a concern as contraband, but nevertheless, the porous borders were seen as a weakness to American integrity. The amendment was ratified in 1919, and several years later, Congress passed the Labor Appropriations Act of 1924, establishing the US Border Patrol.

Also in 1924, Congress passed the Immigration Act, which limited the number of immigrants allowed entry into the United States through a national origins quota.[7] The quota provided immigration visas to 2 percent of the total number of people of each nationality in the United States as of the 1890 national census. It completely excluded immigrants (except Japanese Filipinos) from Asia, which was known as an "Asiatic Barred Zone," because they were not eligible for citizenship. Any nationality ineligible for US citizenship was banned from access to the United States, according to the bill.

The bill was primarily designed to maintain America's homogeneity and not tilt it toward an increase in ethnic diversity with citizens from any particular country. Immigration from the Western Hemisphere was not restricted, and the xenophobic undertones of the debates before the bill's passage became part of the legislation. US Representative Albert Johnson of Washington (chairman of the House Immigration Committee) and author of the bill said during a debate, "It has become necessary that the United States cease to become an asylum."[8]

Initially, the newly established US Border Patrol was charged with patrolling between ports of entry to enforce the immigration policies. By 1925, it could also monitor the coast. The act expanded the Border Patrol to 450 officers from a fluctuating group of about 75 part-time officers. The government initially provided each agent a badge and revolver. Recruits furnished their own horses and saddles, but Washington supplied oats and hay for the horses and a $1,680 annual salary for each agent, with an annual budget of $1 million for the patrol.[9] The agents did not have uniforms until 1928. The majority of the newly formed border security force went to the Canadian border to stop booze smuggling there, but it also scrutinized Mexicans and "threats" from the southern border. The first Border Patrol stations were established in Detroit, Michigan, and El Paso, Texas, both in 1924. By 1930, the Border Patrol force had nearly doubled.[10]

The formation of the Border Patrol was a result of restricting immigrants from non–Latin American countries, but there was still a punitive and racist attitude toward Mexicans at the southern border. There was little immigration from Mexican nationals at this time. Most of the processing at ports of entry was for work visas so people could easily go back and forth between the two countries. In many border towns, Mexicans could pay an annual fee to obtain a work and commerce visa and move legally across the border either way. But when a typhus scare hit the United States in 1916, the inspection process to get into the country from Mexico became downright inhumane.

It was known that fleas and lice carried the disease of typhus, and Mexicans at the inspection station and the port of entry in El Paso were deemed responsible for the outbreak. Even though the Public Health Service officer in the region admitted that there was little danger of typhus being spread by Mexicans, the then mayor of El Paso, Thomas Calloway Lea Jr., was convinced otherwise. He pleaded with Congress to build quarantine stations at the port of El Paso and Juarez to disinfect the "dirty lousey destitute Mexicans."[11]

Congress agreed, and a delousing or quarantine station was installed at the port of entry between El Paso, Texas, and Juarez, Mexico. The idea quickly spread to other ports of entry along the border. All Mexicans were subject to delousing procedures as a requirement to enter the United States, and it became part of the routine inspection process to cross the border. Even those who worked in the United States on a daily basis would have to go through the process every time they entered.

The process of delousing, then, was a daily ritual that served more to debase the border crossers than it did to prevent typhus. The fact that all individuals, male and female alike—including children—had to strip naked and be fumigated caused tensions to rise and sparked one of the first protests against US border control policies in history.

A 1917 account by C. C. Pierce, the senior surgeon for the US Public Health Service at the time, best describes the process for Mexicans entering the United States:

> The men and women are separated, men entering one side of the building and women and small children the other. In suitable rooms all clothing is removed and pushed through an opening in the wall into the disinfecting room, where the bundles are placed in the steam-chamber carriage run out to receive them. Shoes, hats, belts, and other articles injured by

steam are dropped through another opening into a large laundry basket, and when necessary are exposed to cyanogen.[12]

Cyanogen is toxic to humans. It can irritate the eyes and respiratory system. Inhalation can lead to headache, dizziness, rapid pulse, nausea, vomiting, loss of consciousness, convulsions, and death, depending on exposure. Once the men and women stripped down, they would have to pass in front of an inspector and be searched for head lice. If any were found, their heads would be shaved without question; if they didn't want their heads shaved, they could not enter the United States.

There is no accounting of how many people were found with head lice, but if they were, a mixture of acetic acid and kerosene was placed on their heads:

> Women with head lice have a mixture of equal parts of kerosene and vinegar applied to the head and hair for half an hour with a towel covering the head. The dilute acetic acid loosens the eggs from the hair and the kerosene kills or stupefies the adult lice, which are removed by washing the head and hair with warm water and soap. If necessary, the process is repeated to dislodge all eggs or nits. After being passed by the attendant, liquid soap is sprayed upon the body from an elevated reservoir and the person proceeds to the baths.

Even after the delousing process, all individuals were forced to bathe naked, and they were watched as they bathed.

It was a dehumanizing process, and at some point, one woman decided she had had enough. On the morning of January 28, 1917, Carmelita Torres, age seventeen, made her way to the Santa Fe international bridge that connects Juarez, Mexico, with El Paso, Texas. Torres was heading to the port of entry at the end of the bridge as she did most mornings. She was a housekeeper who lived in Juarez and cleaned the homes of the wealthy in El Paso. At the time, Mexicans did not need a visa to work in the United States, but this daily delousing was now mandatory. A seventeen-year-old girl heading to El Paso for work every morning was no exception. That same year, over 127,000 Mexicans would go through delousing at the Santa Fe International Bridge alone.[13]

Torres hated the process. She knew that customs agents photographed women as they undressed and posted the pictures of the nude women on the walls of local bars. And just a few months earlier, sixteen prisoners being bathed in gasoline in an El Paso jail had been burned to death when a lit cigarette ignited it. Given all that, the tension at the border crossing was high.

As Torres approached the customs office, her resolve grew. She could not subject herself to this daily humiliation any longer. She had been building her courage as she waited in line. When she reached the customs agent, she was asked to strip down. This time was different. She refused to take off her clothes. She had convinced thirty other women in line to do the same. A murmur went through the crowd. Within an hour, the protest grew to over two hundred individuals refusing to go through the humiliating delousing process, and by the end of the day, thousands had joined, spilling out onto the streets and bringing the border crossing office to a standstill. Soldiers were called in from nearby Fort Bliss, but they were unable to break up the protesters.[14]

Eventually, Torres was arrested, and the "bath riots," as they came to be known, were brought to an end. Torres became a hero to many. Some call her the Mexican Rosa Parks.[15] As a result of the riots and daily humiliation of the delousing process, Mexicans who had crossed the Santa Fe bridge port of entry began to avoid it altogether. They found other routes and began crossing into El Paso illegally in large numbers. El Paso responded to the high level of illegal entries by instituting mounted patrol agents who monitored the region on horseback. Most were Texas Rangers, who would patrol the border sporadically as needed until the US Border Patrol replaced them at that task several years later.[16]

The typhus scare ended in 1918, but the delousing of Mexicans continued along the border for another forty years.

To summarize, Carmelita Torres had crossed the border legally for work every morning at a job that legal US residents had provided to her, yet the barriers for her to enter legally became so great that she and others decided to protest. As a result, many began to enter illegally.

In the early 1940s, US farms were short on labor as American men joined the World War II effort. Labor from Mexico was the easiest solution. The US and Mexico governments, alongside agribusiness, created a worker program for millions of farmworkers to legally enter the United States and tend to America's crops. The Mexican Farm Labor Agreement of 1942, better known as the Bracero program ("bracero" means "manual laborer"), forever changed the physical face of the United States. About 4.6 million Mexican farmworkers came to the United States between 1942 and 1964, when the program ended. Many farmworkers stayed and set down roots. Many Mexican American neighborhoods in the American Southwest have their origins in the Bracero program.

The Mexican Farm Labor Agreement illustrated the pull of the United States job market and the complicating factors that would push the country to begin to seal the border. Over the span of the several decades of the Bracero program, nearly five million workers migrated to US fields. Some would go back home after the harvest, some would leave the fields to find work in US cities, and some would stay without permission. Many other migrants who could not cobble together the necessary paperwork or did not want to bother with the application process would bypass the rigors of the system and enter the States illegally. Farm owners were all too happy to hire undocumented labor to help keep paperwork and costs down. The US government, for the most part, did not devise an adequate security plan to monitor the workers once they entered. It became too convenient for Mexican farmworkers to stay beyond their work permits, and it became too convenient for workers to fall in love and raise families in the United States.

Working conditions for the farmworkers were deplorable. Carranco Fuentes, a former bracero from the state of Aguascalientes, Mexico, related a story of living conditions in which many farmers were packed into barracks-style housing or overcrowded, rundown apartments. He had been a bracero from 1947 to 1950 and was seventeen when he started. Most of the time, there was no heat, seldom any plumbing, and the rooms were rarely clean. Pay was minimal at about thirty cents an hour, and sometimes deductions came out of his paycheck without explanation. He felt he was treated like cattle, being shoved in and out of housing and being shipped from farm to farm for the harvest without any approval from him.[17] Many who did not speak English or earn enough money to rent homes lived in the farm labor housing that the growers provided. What had begun as a temporary labor shortage program that ended in the sixties became an importation of generations of "cheap" labor from Mexico that continues to this day. A pipeline from Mexico to the agricultural fields in the United States was established and remains entrenched today; many current farm laborers working in the United States are undocumented. Mexican American families can claim their immigrant roots from this time—it is one of the main reasons that the American Southwest has such a large Latino population today.

The recent rise in border walls, an exponential growth in the number of border guards, and a strong militaristic approach to managing the US-Mexico border are recent phenomena. But their roots can be traced to 1986, when President Ronald Reagan signed the Immigration Reform and Control Act into law. The law was initially a response to the waves of undocumented immigrants that were coming to the United States for various issues occurring mostly in Latin America and economic booms in the States that required large amounts of labor. It was also aimed at employers of undocumented labor as a way of restricting people crossing illegally in search of jobs. Before this law, it had generally been legal for employers to hire undocumented immigrants. After its passage, employers who hired them would be subject to civil penalties ranging from $250 to $10,000 for each such violation.[18]

Reagan's "amnesty bill," as some call it, was initially sold as a restriction on illegal immigration. Republicans, Democrats, and the president pushed it through Congress as a provision for increased border security as well as a punitive measure for employers who hired undocumented labor. But Reagan was not sheepish with his vocal support of legalizing the millions of undocumented immigrants who were being exploited and forced to live in the shadows. During a debate with Democratic nominee Walter Mondale in 1984, Reagan said, "I believe in the idea of amnesty for those who have put down roots and lived here, even though sometime back they may have entered illegally." Agriculture lobbies were able to water down employer restrictions and amplify provisions for legalization of those who had lived in the United States for more than ten years.

The legislation stipulated that employers had to verify the legal immigration status of all their employees, and border security would tighten to prevent more immigrants from coming. As a trade-off, those undocumented immigrants who had entered the country before 1982 and remained in the United States continuously since then would qualify for legal permanent residency (sometimes called "getting a green card"). They had an eighteen-month window to apply. To qualify for a green card, in addition to proving residency, immigrants had to have committed no crimes, have knowledge of US history, and demonstrate an understanding of the English language. Nearly three million undocumented immigrants gained legal status with the new law, the vast majority from Mexico.[19]

But the bill did not address the root causes for the migration to the United States in the first place. It placed most of the blame on immigrants for entering the country illegally, without taking into account why they came or the forces that drove them from their countries of origin. And even in deciding to grant amnesty to some immigrants, the bill's authors also made sure to provide for a militaristic approach to border enforcement. The border would be fortified with physical barriers, and more border guards would be deployed. If the United States was going to grant an exception to codified immigration law by granting amnesty, it was going to make sure, by sheer force, that immigrants would not come illegally again.

There were many media accounts of migrants surging toward the United States in the hope that they would qualify for the amnesty program. According to the Border Patrol, there was a spike in illegal attempts to enter the States after the bill's passage; its statistics recorded a rise in apprehensions during the eighteen-month application period for legalization.[20] It is unclear whether there were in fact more illegal attempts to enter the United States; what we do know is that the uptick in apprehensions correlates, in part, to an increase in the size of the US Border Patrol during the same period. Between 1984 and 1985, the Border Patrol grew by almost 700 agents to a total of 3,005—an increase of nearly 30 percent.[21] And beefed-up border security tactics also made it easier for agents to catch would-be migrants.[22] This was the beginning of a pattern of migration booms, followed again by increases in border security.

Detractors of the bill seized upon the uptick in illegal entries and apprehensions. Politicians were sure that many were coming to take part in the amnesty program and that such programs only fueled illegal immigration.

Politicians insisted that the amnesty bill granted legal status to "lawbreakers" and began to make the US-Mexico border central to their political campaigns. Senator Phil Gramm, Republican of Texas, led the opposition. He denounced the bill's amnesty for illegal aliens. In addition, he said it was "outrageous" that under one section, illegal aliens who had done only ninety days of agricultural work in this country could eventually become permanent residents. Mr. Alan Simpson of Wyoming also said he feared that illegal aliens would use fraudulent documents, such as rent receipts and pay stubs, in an effort to show that they had lived here long enough to obtain legal status. Senator Simpson said, "Document fraud is already a cottage industry in America." Senator Pete V. Domenici, a New Mexico Republican, said the bill would "create an administrative nightmare" for employers, who had to ask all job applicants for documents to verify that they were eligible to work in the United States. The bill, he said, was "an invitation to fraud and abuse, an invitation to disaster."[23]

Even though the amnesty portion of the bill was an acknowledgment that migrants had set down roots in the United States and deporting them would separate families, real numbers and facts didn't seem to matter. Hyperbole and rhetoric began to rule the debate, as they would for decades to come.

It wasn't just that immigrants were trying to enter the country illegally, but they were bringing their families, and the population of Latino immigrants in the United States was growing too large for the comfort of some. Their anti-Latino wave showed up in rhetoric that made its way into legislation. Bills for "English only" in schools accompanied campaigns to strengthen the border. In 1985, Kae T. Patrick, a member of the Texas House of Representatives from San Antonio, unsuccessfully pushed a bill to authorize English as the official language of Texas. Patrick said it was more important than having a state bird.[24] A decade later, Governor Pete Wilson ran a reelection campaign on the fear that undocumented immigrants would overrun the state— and he won.[25] There was paranoia, too, that immigrants were crashing the economy. It was easy to scare people into believing that the United States was losing its Anglo/English-speaking heritage. Even though research has proven that amnesty programs do not overall increase the size of the undocumented immigrant population, the drumbeat that there was a need for a secure and militarized border was relentless.[26]

A series of policy decisions that reflected the political backlash marked the years that followed Reagan's amnesty bill. Border security measures such as Operation Gatekeeper in San Diego and Operation Hold the Line in El Paso were, in part, consequences of the touted failures of comprehensive immigration reform. Border security buildup and a drumbeat to deport the undocumented became staples of any immigration reform proposal. No longer would a compassionate view of immigrants lead the debate. Nowhere was this more evident than in California. The state's rich agricultural industry and its housing booms had historically attracted millions of immigrants, many of them from Mexico. Immigrants had been welcome to some degree, and there had been a tacit understanding that the state could not function without them, especially undocumented immigrants, yet fear and rhetoric had grown so loud and strong that it now became politically expedient to target them.

In the early days of 1994, incumbent governor of California Pete Wilson, having already served four years, was trailing in campaign polls leading up to the election by as much as 20 percent against his Democratic challenger, Kathleen Brown.[27] The topic of illegal immigration had been polling well in the state, and Republican Assemblyman Dick Mountjoy of Monrovia had introduced Proposition 187 to its legislature.[28] Mountjoy, a staunch leading California Republican, said he would vow to "stop the illegal alien invasion" at any cost. The ballot initiative seemed to fulfill his wishes. It was known as the "Save Our State" or "SOS" proposition.[29] The initiative would ban all public funds such as those for schools, hospitals, and libraries from providing services to undocumented immigrants. State and local employees could be fined for not asking for proof of legal residency, placing them in the role of immigration police. Local law enforcement would also be required to turn over any immigrants it suspected of being in the country illegally to federal immigration authorities. Polling showed that the proposition was very popular among likely voters, especially Republicans. The strategy of blaming undocumented immigrants for the woes of California was paying off. The incumbent governor took notice.

To save his political career, Governor Pete Wilson doubled down and fully supported Proposition 187 as it made its way through the state legislature. Two-thirds of Californians disapproved of the governor's job performance, yet his staunch support of Prop 187 was a smart political move. Initial polling of community responses showed that Proposition 187 began with widespread support—a thirty-seven-point lead in July 1994 and a 62 percent lead among likely voters.[30] Wilson jumped behind the bill, and his popularity rose.[31] In the days leading up to the election, Wilson vowed that he would put muscle behind the proposed law by requiring all state and local government employees to report "suspected" illegal immigrants to the state attorney general's office. California, led by the unpopular governor, was going to become a police state against immigrants, and government employees would be allowed to profile those they believed to be undocumented. Critics point to a TV ad that helped to scare constituents and push Wilson forward in the polls. A grainy surveillance camera video of migrants running across the border was the centerpiece, with Wilson's voice simply stating, "They keep coming." According to the *Los Angeles Times*, "Wilson seized on the provocative initiative and, through a racist campaign, tapped the latent bigotry of Californians to rescue his flailing candidacy, a Pyrrhic victory that has badly damaged Republicans by alienating Latinos in the state and nationwide ever since."[32]

The then powerless Latino constituency, along with Democrats, protested vehemently but to no avail. Governor Pete

Wilson was reelected for a second term, and voters overwhelmingly accepted Proposition 187. Three days after Wilson signed the bill into law, Federal Judge Matthew Byrne issued a temporary restraining order against the measure. In 1997, Federal Judge Mariana Pfaelzer declared the law unconstitutional based on the fact that states do not carry jurisdiction over federal matters pertaining to immigration.[33] Although the bill was never really implemented, it represented the birth of using the border as successful political rhetoric and immigrants as scapegoats for whatever ailed politicians. According to California Democratic leaders, Proposition 187 and the campaign tactics used to scare voters about immigrants eventually was the undoing of the Republican party in the state. Former California State Democratic Chairman Art Torres said, "Prop 187 was the last gasp of white redneck America."[34] After Wilson's victory, the state made a shift toward a Democratic legislature, and the Latino share of the California electorate rose dramatically.[35] Today, the state is governed by a Democratic legislature and a Democratic governor, with no sign of either turning red in the future. Still, the same anti-immigrant tactics are being used today, most notably by the current Trump administration.

2

The War Begins—Again

When I was a kid growing up within eyeshot of the Mexico border, there was not much of a barrier between the two countries. From my family home, the most prominent natural feature I could see was a flat-topped mesa about a half mile to the south. It separated the river valley I grew up in from Mexico. My friends and relatives would often hike to the top of the mesa to see the spectacular views of the region where the two countries met. To the left of the mesa was Smugglers Gulch, named for a small, tight canyon filled with trees where undocumented immigrants would gain access to the United States every night. To the right was the Pacific Ocean. The surrounding area was a pristine natural environment. There were very few homes—mostly ranch houses, plus farms, horse stables, and a lot of wildlife living in the coastal hills and canyons. The weather was always warm, and in the winter, rain would fill the streams and turn the hillsides green with wild grasses. Our family used to purchase bottled water that came from a natural spring in the

area, and there was a nearby avocado grove. We would fill grocery bags with the fruits. The area was known as the Tijuana
River Valley. Although the river had been named after the city
to the south in Mexico, its mouth was actually in southern San
Diego, and it was my playground.

The steep hike up the rocky cliff to the top of the mesa was
inches from the actual US-Mexico borderline. We could hear
the cars on the highway below us in Mexico. Music came from
the homes of our Mexican neighbors to the south. Trash fires
were common, and we were so close that we could see and
smell them. There was no real fence, no barrier, no line that
defined the transition between the two countries. In places,
there had once been a low chain-link fence, but most of it had
rusted or become overgrown with brush.

At the top of the mesa was a eucalyptus grove, most likely
planted decades or maybe even a century prior. Mature trees
provided cool shade after our uphill climbs. We carved our
names in the trunks of the trees alongside the hearts and promises of love already scarred into them. The trunks provided a
history of visitors to the secluded spot. Most of the writing was
in Spanish, since Mexicans frequently visited the spot as well.
We would bring food and have picnics under the tall trees and
celebrate birthdays. Sometimes we would continue our hikes
to the west, toward the ocean. The Tijuana River emptied into
the Pacific Ocean in San Diego County only a few hundred
yards north of Mexico. There was not much of a fence or barrier
there, either. There was actually a park on top of a hill overlooking the magnificent view of the ocean, and in Mexico, there was
a large bullring stadium. In 1971, First Lady Pat Nixon declared
this area a monument and inaugurated the bluff overlooking the
ocean as Friendship Park. According to Nixon, it was to become
a symbol of binational friendship. Families from Mexico would
gather in the park and picnic with relatives who were living in
the United States. There were meetings, weddings, and birthdays there, and until 1994, there was no fence. You didn't need

a passport or identification in the area. It was like a free zone. There was always a Border Patrol agent or two hovering around, but for the most part, it was a place of unity and tranquil beauty.

Southern California was the destination for undocumented immigrants, and they would gain access to the United States through Tijuana and cross into San Diego. There, it was a reasonably safe place to cross the border. The climate was mild, and there were big cities just up the coast and jobs everywhere. If you were coming into the United States illegally, this is where you wanted to cross. But in the late eighties and early nineties, this pristine area became one of the main centers for the militarization of the border with Mexico. The region would never look—or be—the same again.

- - -

It is widely believed that the border security buildup we see today began as a response to the terrorist attacks of 9/11. It is true that the George W. Bush administration almost doubled the size of the Border Patrol and built seven hundred miles of new border fencing. But the blueprint for a militarized approach, one that caused massive death, began in earnest under the administration of a Democrat, Bill Clinton. The early nineties saw the development of strategies placing never-before-seen infrastructure and tactics that made the southern border look more like a theater of war than a dividing line between two allies.

Clinton had learned from the successes of the heated rhetoric of the political right. He outplayed Republicans by appearing to be tougher on immigrants than they were. They could not run against him on one of their key planks, because he had outdone them. Even though he courted the support of both left-leaning immigrant rights advocates and staunch border enforcement Republicans, his approach was always skewed toward more punitive measures against immigrants, both undocumented and legal. He spent time in office giving speeches that portrayed immigrants as criminals. He built the infrastructure for an undeclared war on immigrants by blocking them at the border and denying their rights in the interior.

Bill Clinton was an astute politician. As the governor of Arkansas, he had had little experience with the issue of immigration, but he was aware of the political payoff that jumping into the immigration debate would offer. He did not want to appear as a neophyte on the global stage. To help make himself look tougher on illegal immigrants and give himself the appearance of having a grasp on a national issue that had the attention of voters, he took what appeared to be a tough, rhetoric-filled militaristic approach to solving the problem.[1]

In 1994, once illegal immigration was a fully entrenched political topic, the Clinton administration began an unprecedented border security buildup. Although Clinton's first bid for the White House rarely mentioned the issue of immigration and it had not yet become a heated political topic, it did not take long for the master politician to use immigration rhetoric to his advantage. It was becoming increasingly popular to point fingers at immigrants, especially those from Mexico, for America's problems. In light of crisis after crisis in Mexico, along with unfair trade practices by the United States that forced mass migration to America, politicians were quick to focus on the numbers of immigrants rather than potential solutions. There was a definite and growing problem, with hundreds of thousands of undocumented immigrants entering the United States, but remedies for the mass migration rarely addressed root causes and therefore had little lasting effect. Mexico's economy was suffering, and the instability of its government was growing, causing a mass exodus to the United States. Yet American policies were primarily based on walling off the migration, not alleviating the problems that led to it.

In December 1993, Clinton signed the North American Free Trade Agreement. The deal aimed to increase trade and manufacturing between Canada, the United States, and Mexico.

The agreement was sold as an economic boon to all countries involved. Mexico, in particular, was going to receive billions of dollars in investment for manufacturing and agriculture, and millions of new jobs were promised. The agreement had the opposite effect. Over a short period after the agreement was enacted, Mexico's peso was devalued, creating a currency crisis; produce prices dropped, and China began to underbid global manufacturing.

Heavily subsidized US corn flooded south of the border, drastically dropping the price of corn in Mexico.[2] Food prices rose. Notably, the price for tortillas, a staple in Mexico, shot up. The assassination of a presidential candidate and an uprising by native poor farmworkers in the state of Chiapas against the seizure of their land contributed to the sense of instability throughout the country. Unemployment climbed from 3.9 percent at its precrisis level in 1994 to 7.4 percent in 1995. In the formal sector alone—those who work a traditional forty-hour workweek and earn a regular paycheck—over one million people lost their jobs. It is estimated that two million farmworkers also lost their jobs. At the same time, average real wages decreased by 13.5 percent throughout 1995. Overall household incomes plummeted by 30 percent in the same year. Mexico's extreme poverty grew from 21 percent in 1994 to 37 percent in 1996, undoing the previous ten years of successful poverty reduction initiatives. The nation's poverty levels would not begin returning to normal until 2001.[3]

Mexico's economic recession kept a steady stream of migrants heading for the United States. It is estimated that at the recession's peak, over one million people a year were illegally crossing the border into the States.[4] Illegal crossings caught the attention of lawmakers and made the border a national issue. No longer was California alone in feeling the effects of migration.

Images of people crossing the border and fleeing joblessness and a weakening economy appeared on the nightly news. Migrants by the hundreds would take to the freeways, running between vehicles so they would be hard to apprehend. They ran in large packs to find safety in numbers; only a few would get caught. Hundreds of people ran for their lives every night, and the media was happy to show this to viewers.

Over a hundred immigrants were killed in collisions on California roads between 1987 and 1990.[5] A US highway safety sign was actually created to be posted near the US-Mexico border to warn motorists of immigrants running on freeways. The bright-yellow sign carried black silhouettes of a man, a woman, and a girl with pigtails, running. The sign appeared to depict a family racing across the road much in the same way as cattle or deer crossing signs do. Other signs read, "Caution WATCH FOR PEOPLE CROSSING ROAD." The road signs did not prove to be enough, and the *Los Angeles Times* reported, "Caltrans to Build I-5 Safety Fence: Migrants: The $3-million center divider near the Camp Pendleton checkpoint is designed to keep illegal aliens from being killed on the freeway."[6]

Poverty—in part driven by US trade policy—was the root cause of the influx of immigrants from Mexico. Instead of addressing the cause, politicians, including Governor Pete Wilson in California, were happy to champion tough and punitive policies toward immigrants. Even the president had taken notice. Bill Clinton had the power to fortify the border and increase the number of guards. As I've noted, over the course of his first term, he did that and much more.

- - -

In 1992, the George H. W. Bush administration ordered a study on how best to manage illegal narcotics entering the United States. As part of the National Drug Control Strategy study, Sandia National Laboratories focused on the US-Mexico border and weaknesses where smugglers had easy access to the United States.[7] The study also included a technical analysis of possible border fence infrastructure that could deter both illegal immigration and drug smugglers. That part of the study was referred to as "The Systematic Analysis of the Southwest Border."

Sandia National Laboratories had grown out of the World War II effort to develop the first atomic bombs and the Manhattan Project. Since then, it has become a national laboratory designated by the US Congress and serves primarily as a privately run defense contractor and think tank to manage the United States' nuclear arsenal as well as to strategize how best to manage zones of conflict around the world—even the US-Mexico border. In the past, Sandia was managed by AT&T, and then by Lockheed Martin. It is currently managed by National Technology and Engineering Solutions of Sandia, a wholly owned subsidiary of Honeywell International. Sandia currently receives $2.4 billion in contracts from the federal government.[8]

Sandia was asked to study the border and make recommendations to the federal government and US Border Patrol on how to stop the illegal flow of people and contraband. The recommendations were very specific, with detailed drawings of border fences, and included a militaristic approach to the issues of migration confronting the American Southwest border. For the first time in American history, the United States was going to have a substantial warlike footing on the border and to use its troops on the ground to defend itself from (at the time) mostly Mexicans—mostly economic migrants.

It is important to acknowledge that drug dealers and criminals were easily gaining access to the United States from points south, but the newly proposed maze of border security infrastructure would have to be navigated by laborers as well. People who had been coming to the United States for years for seasonal and temporary work would be subject to a militarized infrastructure. Sandia's recommendations to the Department of Justice were to defend America from all who attempted to cross the border illegally, even if they were poor farmworkers hired by US agricultural interests. Border security infrastructure would be increased, along with the personnel and technology to man it. Not all recommendations were implemented, but the idea of building a warlike front—designed by a military contractor—would be the approach for decades to come.

The Sandia study advocated for a triple-layer border fence along the border in cities like San Diego and El Paso. The pristine natural setting where I grew up was going to be the first place that this three-layer fence would be implemented. The zone where the two countries met and slightly merged would have a hard line drawn across it. Friendship Park was to be sealed off forever.

The triple-layer fence would work as follows. At the physical borderline itself, there would be a ten-foot opaque wall. Just north of it, between that wall and the second, there would be a road for Border Patrol vehicle access. The second, middle wall was dubbed the First DeFence (get it?). It would be a curved wall fifteen feet tall, constructed of heavy-gauge Weldmesh. Beyond that would be another road, and then the third fence—ten feet tall.[9] In other words, if someone tried to scale the first border wall, he or she would be faced with two more beyond it, with access roads and vehicles patrolling the area. Just the sheer sight of the metal maze would, the report predicted, be enough to scare off any migrant.

Some of the Sandia study recommendations were already being tested in San Diego by the time the report was sent to the Office of National Drug Control Policy in 1993. Fencing had been constructed around Friendship Park and by the Pacific Ocean, making it impossible for families to meet as they had in the past in this once-sanctified free zone. The San Diego Border Patrol sector began an initiative to erect stronger physical barriers in 1990. About fourteen miles of ten-foot welded-steel fencing was installed along the border where the patrol believed that most unauthorized crossings of drugs and people occurred.[10] Border Patrol claimed that the fence was working, because apprehensions were down in the area where it had been implemented.

But there was also evidence that migration had simply been shunted to points east, away from the infrastructure buildup, as apprehensions had spiked where there was no fencing.

In rural areas away from cities, the border security patrolling needed to be different. According to one Border Patrol agent quoted in an Office of Inspector General report, migrants would just search for more open and rugged terrain away from the fencing.[11] Building fencing along the entirety of the southern border was impossible due to mountainous terrain, lack of roads, and the sheer cost of covering its nearly two thousand miles. The wide-open spaces and topography posed challenges that were to be addressed with military-style equipment and tactics. In open, less populated areas along the border, surveillance or sensor systems would be deployed. There would be a heavy reliance on ground sensors, night vision capability, heat and motion sensors, cameras, surveillance towers, and helicopters. Information from the sensors and technology would alert Border Patrol agents on the ground who then could theoretically intercept any would-be border crossers.

In addition to reliance on technology in places away from the cities, the recommendations included concrete vehicle barriers and movable and static checkpoints. Any vehicles entering the country would be stopped, and people would be asked about their legal residency status. Sandia was advocating for federal agents to stop US citizens and others, all on the suspicion that they might be undocumented. Everyone would become a suspect. This was an unprecedented suggestion fraught with Fourth Amendment violations. The ACLU argued, "The Fourth Amendment to the U.S. Constitution protects against arbitrary searches and seizures of people and their property, even in this expanded border area. And, depending on where you are in this area and how long an agent detains you, agents must have varying levels of suspicion to hold you."[12] The ACLU, along with other organizations, filed numerous lawsuits against the tactics used at such checkpoints, with most verdicts siding with the federal government. Cases included suits against the federal government's authority to establish checkpoints in the first place, because there was not sufficient probable cause to stop motorists just because they were in proximity of the US-Mexico border. The ACLU also filed suits against the Border Patrol for boarding public buses in search of undocumented immigrants at these checkpoints.

In addition, Sandia recommended penalties for so-called repeat offenders (those who had been deported previously) and recommended they suffer harsher consequences, which were labeled "deep" deportation.[13] This meant that if someone was caught reentering the United States after being deported, he or she would be sent to a region of Mexico far from his or her home. The hope was that if the journey back home was difficult, someone would think twice about trying to come back to the United States. Although the recommended strategies for deterring migrants would not be published for another year, the concept of making a border crossing as difficult as possible appears to have had its roots here. The Sandia recommendations assured that migrants would suffer if they were caught entering the United States. This kind of strategy would be expanded upon and continues to be enhanced through the Trump administration today.

Most of the recommendations in the report were the harshest ever considered by the government, but they did not all originate with Sandia. In fact, many of the strategies that Sandia adopted had already been published in a paper by the Federation for American Immigration Reform (FAIR) in 1989. FAIR is a Southern Poverty Law Center–designated hate group and has been known since its founding in 1979 as an immigration restrictionist organization. Leaders of the organization have known ties to white supremacy groups. According to the Southern Poverty Law Center, "Although FAIR maintains a veneer of legitimacy that has allowed its principals to testify in Congress and lobby the federal government, this veneer hides much ugliness."[14]

In the words of the founder of FAIR, John Tanton, in 1988, "As Whites see their power and control over their lives declining, will they simply go quietly into the night? Or will there be an explosion?" The 1989 FAIR study "Ten Steps to Securing America's Borders" was conducted by a retired head of the US Border Patrol, and it recommended adding vehicle barriers, checkpoints, and enhanced electronic surveillance equipment as well as a triple-layer border fence, all of which were reflected in the Sandia report.[15] To date, there is no evidence to prove that Sandia took on the recommendations directly from FAIR, but the similarities in the reports are striking. Deterring migration and smuggling by making the journey difficult and possibly deadly was on its way to becoming US policy.

Initially the Sandia report remained classified, but after it was issued to the Office of National Drug Control Policy, it became the blueprint for border fortification in San Diego and El Paso beginning in 1994. Although not all its recommendations were adopted wholesale, the idea of creating an impenetrable barrier at the US-Mexico border has been implemented in one form or another by all administrations since the report was issued, and every year, the border looks more and more like a militarized zone.

- - -

The accelerated militarization of the border began in response to the Sandia report. At the same time, however, the Clinton administration ordered the US Border Patrol to put together its own report and recommendations. That report, *Border Patrol Strategic Plan 1994 and Beyond—National Strategy*, came to be known as the prevention through deterrence strategy, and it is still being employed today. The Trump administration has garnered a reputation for being "tough on border security," but Congress has enacted no new immigration laws giving President Trump more power than previous presidents. Instead, the administration is merely employing and enforcing laws already enacted during the Clinton years. The policies of deterrence are by far the most consequential policy changes at the border used by all presidents since Clinton.

The prevention through deterrence report and ensuing strategy were supposed to be a part of a larger immigration package that included both border security and a comprehensive look at the entire US immigration system, according to Doris Meissner, the commissioner of Immigration and Naturalization Service (INS) during the Clinton administration who commissioned the Border Patrol report. "There can't be a sealing of the border without looking at a better legal immigration system. The two go hand in hand," Meissner explained when I spoke to her in 2007. "The border region is not a rigid system; we need to find a way to have people move freely and legally," she added.[16]

It is true that a comprehensive approach to immigration reform never made it out of Congress. The executive branch is charged with enforcing immigration laws that Congress passes, a responsibility based on the idea that immigration relates to a matter of sovereignty and that therefore immigration matters can also affect national security. Laws on the books, no matter how old or how they have been enforced in the past, can be implemented by incoming presidents—or not enforced by the decision of the executive branch. In practice, the most significant measures that Bill Clinton approved were punitive ones. The border was sealed more than it ever had been before; no effort was made to offset the reasons that people were coming in the first place, and it got harder—not easier—for people to legalize their immigration status.

With the 1994 Strategic Plan, US Border Patrol leadership concluded that with the manpower available and given the rugged terrain in the American Southwest, there was no way the Border Patrol would ever be able to seal the border outright. The planners did believe, however, that the border region and illegal immigration could "be brought under control."[17] In 1994 the new Border Patrol strategy seemed to be a veiled assault against Mexicans. There were about four thousand agents patrolling the borders of the United States. By the end of the Clinton administration and implementation of the Strategic Plan, that number would more than double; by the end of the George W. Bush administration, it would more than double again, to about twenty thousand agents. The Strategic Plan was initially implemented using the agents already employed and placing them in strategic areas along the border, but as time went on, more agents were called for to secure it.[18]

The new strategy signed by Doris Meissner and approved by the Clinton administration relied on one key addition to the Sandia recommendations: the patrol would use the terrain to its advantage. Since Border Patrol admitted that it could not seal the border between the ports of entry given the size of its forces and resources, the deserts of the American Southwest would serve as the deterrent. The Border Patrol's detailed maps indicated that most migrants attempted to cross into the United States in and near urban areas such as El Paso and San Diego. The plan was to disrupt those traditional and relatively safe routes by concentrating border patrol forces there. If migrants found it too difficult to cross in and near the cities, they would be forced out into open terrain. It was believed that the harsh desert land and climate might even be as effective a deterrent as armed border guards.

This, then, was the new "prevention through deterrence" strategy. Again, it seemed to be a veiled assault against Mexicans: Border Patrol statistics at the time claimed that "97 percent of all aliens were Mexican Nationals."[19] The demographic study within the report seemed to sympathize with the class of people who were crossing; the fact that the strategy would prove to be the most punitive and deadly is almost macabre. The report states, "Typically an alien arrested by the Border Patrol is under the age of 25. Twenty percent are women and children who are attempting to reach their husbands/fathers who are already in the United States. Most of the aliens encountered are poor, are looking for work and have incurred transportation and smugglers' fees."

The report makes the claim that the proposed tactic of prevention through deterrence could push the migrants to "find themselves in mortal danger." There was a clear understanding that a large of portion of the migrants attempting to cross were young and women and children—and this awareness was somehow coupled with the strategy of forcing a vulnerable population through migration routes that included hostile terrain. The foreknowledge that those affected would be young people and women and children did not seem to temper the risks to human life that the strategy proposed; it seemed perfectly logical to place these human beings at risk of dying. "The Border Patrol [would] improve control of the border by implementing a strategy of 'prevention through deterrence.'" According to the report, the tactic would "raise the risk of apprehension to the point that many will consider it futile to continue to attempt illegal entry." So the plan was, given the resources available, the terrain left to the migrants would be inhospitable enough to help control the border. The report stated, "It is necessary to increase the 'cost' to illegal entrants to the point of deterring repeated attempts. As we reduce the rate of recidivism in the illegal entering population, the number of aliens attempting illegal entry will decrease."

The strategy contained an alert that agents must be on the lookout for and try to reduce "serious accidents involving aliens on highways, trains, drowning, dehydration." The proposed strategy even suggested that the "main effort" of reducing migrant strife would be to "watch for the signs of dehydration," meaning that migrants were going to cross the deserts, and dehydration would be their number one foe. After implementation of the strategy, dehydration or "exposure" was the top cause of migrant death, and it continues to be so to this day. Even though the "mortal danger" aspect of the plan has been realized by now, it has not been changed to mitigate death.[20]

The measure of success for the new Border Patrol–generated strategy would be just how many migrants chose to cross elsewhere. If more traffic was forced into the deserts and open areas, then that would keep the urban areas safe. That is, a shift in migration patterns would be a sign that the new strategy was effective. And that is exactly what happened. Migrants began to cross in regions where they never had before. Deserts and mountains were the new routes. The Border Patrol found the strategy of deterrence effective and decided to increase the number of regions where it deployed the new tactics: it expanded the regions where migrants were forced into areas that would make them suffer and possibly die.

The buildup of Border Patrol agents and border walls, first in El Paso and later in San Diego, took its own destructive turn. Operation Hold the Line had begun in September 1993 and was to be built at the border between El Paso and Juarez. This was where illegal crossings were estimated at eight thousand individuals a day. Initially, the name was to be Operation Blockade, but that was dropped due to the negative connotation.[21] Prior to Operation Hold the Line, migrants could easily cross the Rio Grande, and Border Patrol agents would try to apprehend them once they made it to El Paso. The strategy wasn't a popular one in the city, which was overrun by patrol cars and agents always on the chase. Complaints about Border Patrol agents targeting legal residents were rampant, since El Paso is a predominantly Latino community. The new strategy placed agents right along the river in an effort to keep migrants from entering the city at all.

When the new strategy of "prevention through deterrence" took effect, Operation Hold the Line ramped up. Border Patrol agents began using low-flying helicopter patrols to apprehend migrants and built up fencing between the city of El Paso and Juarez, Mexico. Generators and lights were brought in to help agents see would-be crossers at night.[22] Originally the Army Corps of Engineers had built the fence from surplus steel, and the Department of Defense maintained it. As more sophisticated technology was called for, defense contractors like Boeing, Lockheed, and Raytheon began to bid for the ever-increasing border security budgets.

Border Patrol was quick to claim that the operation was successfully reducing attempts by migrants to cross the border. El Paso Sector Border Patrol chief Silvestre Reyes became something of a local hero for getting the border in his region under control. Almost immediately the residents and merchants in El Paso noticed a change. The eight thousand migrants who would try to gain access to El Paso daily were being deterred and forced away from the city. Statistics prove that surrounding sectors in Texas saw an increase in apprehensions, and overall apprehensions border-wide were up after Operation Hold the Line was implemented.[23] There were also claims that Border Patrol agents had been told to count less on apprehensions to make it look like these operations were successful. Agents were instructed to deport migrants without filling out the necessary paperwork or to apprehend only a certain number of migrants per day that so the statistics would indicate that apprehensions were down.[24]

What the Border Patrol didn't overly publicize was the uptick in migrant deaths after Operation Hold the Line began.[25] With all the force concentrated around the city of El Paso, including the bridges, to gain access to the United States, migrants had to swim across the Rio Grande River. The number of migrants who drowned during the crossing increased. According to a US Government Accountability Office report, migrant deaths doubled across the border as well as in Texas the year following the implementation of Operation Hold the Line.[26] It is also important to note that many of the drowning deaths that occur in the Rio Grande are recovered by Mexican officials on their side of the border and not counted in official US totals.

The touted success of the first operation in El Paso increased support for the San Diego efforts, which would soon be called Operation Gatekeeper. There was great support for increased border security, as politicians had scared most of the public into believing that the United States and especially California were being invaded. There was opposition, but it was limited mostly to activists as they began to see a spike in migrant deaths. Only a couple of years after Operation Gatekeeper was implemented, Claudia Smith, an attorney for the California Rural Legal Assistance, became one of the first voices to criticize Operation Gatekeeper and the border security buildup. She publicized the spike in deaths and documented the migration routes that had shifted to more treacherous terrain, but there was no change in policy.[27]

On October 1, 1994, the Clinton administration launched Operation Gatekeeper partially on the heels of the seeming early success of Operation Hold the Line in El Paso. In California, the operation was a response to fast-growing anti-immigrant sentiment in the state, as California was quickly becoming a majority-minority population state. Operation Gatekeeper initially concentrated on the area between the cities of San Diego and Tijuana, which was the most heavily trafficked region for unauthorized migration along the entire border.[28] A new border wall was constructed of corrugated metal sheets, accompanied by a doubling of the Border Patrol force in the area; the increase in force was made visible with the placement of agents at strategic and known crossing routes. In addition, the operation deployed high-intensity stadium lights, heat sensors, helicopters, and infrared telescopes.

Although apprehensions dropped dramatically along the San Diego sector, they spiked eastward, further proving that migration didn't stop; its routes were just changing location. Apprehensions may have been down at the specific ports of entry where the new operations were being implemented, but apprehension rates border-wide were noticeably up by several hundred thousand annually. As a direct result of purposely funneling migration through treacherous terrain, the San Diego region alone also saw a spike in migrant deaths. In 1994, there were fewer than 30 deaths in the California desert; by 1998, that number had increased fivefold to 147 deaths. Migrants now were not just crossing in California deserts; some migration routes had pushed as far east as Arizona. By 2001, the death toll in the California desert reached 387 and would continue to escalate.[29]

Migrant deaths due to the policies of deterrence were not in the public consciousness for several years after the implementation of Operation Gatekeeper and Operation Hold the Line. Although there was some documentation of the effects of migration flows through the deserts and mountains and a spike in migrant death was noted, a humanitarian response did not happen until the death toll began to climb. It took the public a few years to catch up with the fact that people were dying in large numbers. Neither Water Station in California nor Humane Borders (which services most of the Arizona desert by putting out water for migrants) came into existence until the year 2000. No More Deaths, an organization in Arizona dedicated to preventing migrant death, began in 2004. By then, over a thousand migrant bodies had been recovered in the Arizona desert. Similar responses and humanitarian efforts began after the death tolls along the border had reached astronomical numbers.

- - -

The effects of Operations Hold the Line and Gatekeeper affected all those who lived along the US-Mexico border. Some doubled down on law-and-order policies, but others became unlikely activists. In 2005, I met brothers Duncan and John Hunter. Duncan Hunter was a US congressman elected to office in the Fifty-Second District of California in 1980. A former decorated Vietnam vet, he was an adamant proponent of a secure border using military-style tactics. His district neared the US-Mexico border in San Diego, and he had felt a need to get the border "under control," as he said to me. John Hunter had been his brother's primary fundraiser for his bids in Congress. A former rocket scientist, John eventually witnessed the effects of Border Patrol strategy firsthand and decided he needed to act.

Congressman Duncan Hunter had been a strong proponent of Operation Hold the Line in El Paso and was one of the officials pushing the federal government to try a similar tactic in San Diego. He had demanded that the INS put enough agents on the San Diego border to create an El Paso–like human blockade on the border. He had also pushed for more fencing.[30] Hunter would attend any and every congressional hearing about the issue of border security. He would bring fellow politicians to the region and show them an area of the border filled with trash and broken fences.[31] He had quickly become known as a man with a solution for border security, and his approach and answer to the dilemma of migration was purely militaristic.

I had the opportunity to speak with Hunter in his office in Washington, DC, in 2006; by that point, Operation Gatekeeper had been up and running for over ten years, and the effects were pronounced. Hunter would have liked to focus on the fence as a success story. He had had before and after pictures in his office of the San Diego border region since the implementation of Operation Gatekeeper. To him, the border looked better and more controlled with a well-built fence running through it. He was very proud of the photos. In the before photo, there was no border fence, but there was a lot of trash, including food wrappers and beer bottles. In the after photo, the trash was gone, and in its place was a tall border fence made of metal. The after picture had been taken during the winter, when rains had greened up the hillsides, creating a more beautiful and tranquil image. Fences just made things better, according to Hunter.

Hunter thought a fence was the answer to all the border problems. If there was illegal immigration in any part of the border, there should be a fence. If people were dying by crossing the border in the deserts or mountains, there should be a fence blocking access to the dangerous terrain. If migrants were compromising existing fences and border security barriers, the barriers should be strengthened. Fences could be built taller and stronger if necessary. Barriers to migration were the answer to stop illegal immigration. I asked him whether he believed that his advocacy for a border fence had forced migrants to cross elsewhere, ultimately leading to more deaths. In response, he said, "If all those people who are concerned with people dying—and I am concerned with people dying, my brother even puts water out in the desert for people who are dying and he has saved thousands of lives—if those people are so concerned with people dying at the border, why are they against putting a border fence across the whole border? Why don't they want to fence off Arizona or Texas?"[32] His solution to the problems caused by Operation Gatekeeper was to build more barriers to migration. His philosophy was fences to prevent people from coming and fences to prevent people from dying by preventing them from entering the deserts in the first place.

John Hunter, Duncan's brother, worked for Lawrence Livermore National Laboratories at the time.[33] He generally held the same beliefs as his brother: that drug dealers and other criminals were crossing the border and that they should be stopped. Since his brother Duncan was so involved with border security, John also had a fascination with the human drama of migration, and since he had the mind of a scientist, as a side hobby, he researched the best ways to deter migrant traffic. John said that he had designed weapon systems for theaters of war, so how hard could it be to tinker with border security? He would often ride along with Border Patrol agents in the California desert, studying the best ways to fence off the region and prevent migrant traffic. He had reviewed the Sandia study and thought about how best to implement the border security strategy it outlined—or maybe he could devise something better. His analysis would prove useful to Duncan in determining which policies he would propose and support. When I met him, though, he told me about an experience that had changed his perspective about border security altogether.

While John was riding along with border agents one day in 1999, he spotted what looked like other Border Patrol agents off in the distance, arresting a group of migrants. With John in tow, they drove closer to investigate. John had never seen an arrest of migrants before. He was suspecting thugs, drug dealers, or heavily armed brown-faced men. He was expecting to come across the criminal element he was convinced was crossing the border every night. Instead, when the vehicle he was in pulled up, John was shocked to see a group of mature women with their purses sitting on the ground and their backs up against the patrol car. Each one was handcuffed. John recalled, "They were all dressed like they were going to church. They were all dressed up."

The scene hit John hard. He felt responsible. He believed he had had a significant hand in helping his brother get elected and so had some responsibility for helping to build the border wall that had pushed migrants to these deserts. It wasn't until he saw these women that the reports of the spike in migrant deaths finally made him pay attention. He felt he needed to do something.

John began spending his weekends devising strategies to place gallon bottles of water in the desert instead of building better border security. He was the only one in the country doing it at the time, and he created a system that would be copied by other humanitarian groups along the border, including Humane Borders, Samaritans, and No More Deaths. Every weekend, he would load up his truck and grab a few volunteers, usually including his wife, Laura, and their kids. They would spend the weekend finding strategic places where water should be left for migrants. He placed water bottles in large blue plastic trash can–like containers, with lids on to keep wildlife and the elements from affecting the water. Next to each container, John and the volunteers would raise a tall pole with an orange-and-blue flag that migrants could see for miles. Dehydration was a key risk listed in the document approved by the head of the INS

and by the Clinton administration, yet there had been no efforts
to keep migrants from becoming dehydrated and dying.

To this date, the United States itself provides no water for
migrants along dangerous routes. John Hunter and other activists like him were fighting alone to save lives. Hundreds of bodies were being recovered in the deserts of California due to the
deterrence policy adopted by the Clinton administration and
championed by Congressman Duncan Hunter. John and his
crew of volunteers were in a race against time, the elements,
and even his own brother.

- - -

With the touted success of the operations under way in El Paso
and San Diego, Operation Safeguard began in the Fall of 1994
along the Mexico border south of Tucson, Arizona. The initial
plan had always been to use San Diego and El Paso as proving grounds for the operations and, if those were successful,
to continue to roll out implementation of the strategy where
needed. This operation, like those in El Paso and San Diego,
was designed to funnel migration away from busy ports of entry
like Nogales and Douglas, Arizona, and out to more open terrain. Border Patrol agents had produced an in-house training
video, which I received a copy of, highlighting the advantages
of funneling migrants through the desert. In the video, the nar-
rator states that leaving migrants to wander in the open deserts
gave the Border Patrol a "tactical advantage."

The number of agents increased fourfold over a six-year
period—from 282 to over 1,000[34] in the region—and the show of
force seems to have successfully protected the ports of entry in
what was known as the Tucson Sector. The Border Patrol there
also received new surveillance equipment as well as high-intensity
lighting and helicopter surveillance, all provided by defense contractors. The only routes left for crossings were the scorching
deserts and mountains away from civilization. The tightening of

the border along the Tucson Sector proved to be the deadliest of all the operations and did little to reduce migration.

Migrant deaths had been an unknown phenomenon in the region before 1994, but that quickly changed. The migrant death toll skyrocketed in Arizona from 14 documented deaths in 1994 and 11 in 1998 to 90 in 2000, 145 in 2001, and more than 163 in 2002.[35] In 2012, retired Tucson Border Patrol sector chief Ron Sanders critiqued the operation in an interview for *The Nation* magazine, saying, "By every measure, the strategy is a failure. All it's accomplished is killing people." He continued, "But since these people are Mexicans, no one seems to care."[36]

It didn't seem to matter whether the strategies succeeded or how many migrants died. In the summer of 1997, the US Border Patrol launched Operation Rio Grande, centered in the McAllen and Laredo, Texas, sectors. The tactics and results were the same. With both Operation Hold the Line and Operation Rio Grande up and running, the deaths of unauthorized migrants increased from 100 in 1998 to 164 in 2000 for the entire Texas border.[37]

- - -

The Clinton administration's strategy to keep immigration at bay and remain tough at the border never really succeeded in its professed aims. Migrants continued to cross—the deterrence part of the strategy never did work. Just a few years after the implementation of Operation Gatekeeper and the other operations, the number of apprehensions across the border continued to rise. Although apprehensions near the newly fortified parts of the border might have dropped, overall, numbers increased. In 1994, the year in which the operations were implemented, there were 979,101 apprehensions along the entire border. In 1995, there were 1,271,390, and in 1996, there were over 1,507,000.[38] Records were broken year after year after the tightening of border security, and at the same time, the casualties were mounting. Yet the militarization of the border continued as if none of this mattered. And it didn't.

In the early nineties, it was politically popular to be anti-immigrant. As noted earlier, Pete Wilson, the then governor of California, made a miraculous comeback after trailing in the polls by more than twenty points on a tough stance against immigrants. Diane Feinstein, now a DACA advocate and liberal senator from California, had run against undocumented immigrants in her 1994 reelection bid. In her campaign ad that year, she claimed that she had only been in the Senate a short time but had already helped to secure the border with more agents, fencing, lighting, and other equipment.[39] The ad ended with Feinstein looking directly into the camera and stating, "I have just begun to fight for California." Images of immigrants "storming" the border made national news and scared the general population. Words like "invasion" and the state being "overrun" and "drained" of social services accompanied the images. Immigrants were portrayed as coming to the United States to take jobs, commit crimes, and rob Americans of their Social Security benefits and health care.

Clinton was gaining in reputation for being tough on immigrants, and his policies proved it. Although he campaigned on the left as being open-minded about amending the broken legal immigration system, he did very little to relax quotas or laws to allow more immigrants into the country. The laws passed during his tenure did very little to address or alleviate the burdens that are the root causes of migration but instead placed harsh penalties on immigrants both legal and illegal. Punitive measure after punitive measure pointed fingers at immigrants as they were stripped of social services and forced to endure reduced civil liberties. New, restrictive immigration laws would soon follow punitive measures at the border. It almost didn't matter what new immigration laws passed as long as they appeared to be tough on immigrants. That was the popular political climate, and politicians, including the president, portrayed themselves as tough on immigrants to score political points.

In Clinton's first bid for the White House in 1992, the centrist Democrat ran on creating jobs and looking out for the working-class folk of the United States. He wanted to restore America's core values and portrayed himself as a president who would be compassionate and understood the ills of society. The Democratic Party's platform on immigration was no different. It was compassionate toward America's newcomers and supported creating a welcoming society. Just a year into his presidency, however, Clinton began to see a tougher stance on immigrants as a political winner. His rhetoric became sharper, and his support for tough measures at the border and against immigrants was noticeable both in word and policy. By his 1995 State of the Union address, Clinton had adopted the political strategy of immigrant bashing wholeheartedly, and his presidency from then on would reflect it. He said then:

> All Americans, not only in the states most heavily affected but in every place in this country, are rightly disturbed by the large numbers of illegal aliens entering our country. The jobs they hold might otherwise be held by citizens or legal immigrants. The public service they use impose burdens on our taxpayers. That's why our administration has moved aggressively to secure our borders more by hiring a record number of new border guards, by deporting twice as many criminal aliens as ever before, by cracking down on illegal hiring, by barring welfare benefits to illegal aliens. In the budget I will present to you, we will try to do more to speed the deportation of illegal aliens who are arrested for crimes, to better identify illegal aliens in the workplace. . . . We are a nation of immigrants. But we are also a nation of laws. It is wrong and ultimately self-defeating for a nation of immigrants to permit the kind of abuse of our immigration laws we have seen in recent years, and we must do more to stop it.[40]

In 1996, Clinton signed the Personal Responsibility and Work Opportunity Act. The bill dramatically changed the nation's welfare system, now requiring work in exchange for time-limited assistance.[41] Recipients of welfare benefits would have to show that they were working or at least looking for a job. In addition, the bill eliminated any form of access to the welfare system by legal immigrants for the first five years of residency in the United States.[42] It was designed to punish immigrants mostly because they were seen as invading the country and draining its social services, such as welfare. Accounts of any such abuse were anecdotal at best, yet the president felt it necessary to bar even legal immigrants from accessing welfare for five years. Undocumented immigrants, despite the rhetoric from the right saying the opposite, have never been able to access social services without proper identification—so the rumors of "illegals" on welfare are also unfounded.

Clinton also signed the Anti-Terrorism and Effective Death Penalty Act (AEDPA) into law in 1996 as a response to the World Trade Center and Oklahoma City bombings. The act basically allowed the federal government to increase prosecutions and arrests of suspected terrorists. The act also denied immigrants, legal or otherwise, of due process if they were convicted of an aggravated felony. Immigrants of any status could be apprehended and detained without due process. As a result of this law, the number of immigrants in detention doubled in two years—from 8,500 in 1996 to nearly 16,000 in 1998.[43] Again, the law seemed to send a message that immigrants were criminal in nature and needed to be detained. It also created a belief that immigrants did not deserve full representation under the law. Immigrants could be subject to harsher penalties and longer detention periods than citizens who might have committed the same crimes. Immigrants, again, were to be watched, warily.

The Illegal Immigration Reform and Immigrant Responsibility Act of 1996 (IIRIRA) also received Clinton's signature and drastically changed the way that the United States managed its policies and controlled immigrants. The law placed restrictions of up to ten years if undocumented immigrants were caught in the country without documents. This meant that if an undocumented immigrant was deported, he or she could not apply for any legal means to enter the country for at least ten years.[44] The result of the policy caused families of mixed immigration status to be separated. For example, if the head of a household was an undocumented father of US citizen children and had an undocumented wife, and he was deported, IIRIRA would not allow him legal access or even to apply for it for up to ten years—a long time to remain separated from his family. The bill was designed to discourage illegal immigration by placing such burdensome penalties on those that would dare to enter it that way. In many cases, however, it had the opposite effect. If this father was deported and faced such a long separation from his family, he would most likely attempt to enter the country illegally, because there was just no other legal means to reunite with his family.

"Before President Clinton took office, enforcement of our immigration laws and an up-to-date immigration policy had been absent for nearly a decade," said Leon E. Panetta in 1996, the White House chief of staff at that time. "The Clinton Administration has developed a comprehensive anti-illegal immigration policy that beefs up our border and workplace enforcement inspections and has used the criminal justice system to deport a record number of criminals and other illegal aliens."[45] According to Panetta, the war on immigrants in the interior was matching the war on immigrants at the border.

The IIRIRA opened the door to the kinds of punitive policies and procedures we witness being used today even by the Trump administration. The law gave the executive branch great authority over border security and allowed for the construction of border walls along the US-Mexico border or to fortify existing ones. The law also allowed the attorney general's office to interact with local law enforcement on immigration matters.

The 287g provision of the law could, in effect, deputize local law enforcement as federal immigration officers. Now, county sheriffs' departments and municipal police could ask suspected undocumented immigrants for proof of legal residency.[46] The measure sent shock waves of fear through immigrant communities. People stopped trusting local police and reporting crimes for fear of deportation. Cops could now become immigration agents.

The law also limited undocumented immigrants' access to the higher-education system in the United States by restricting states from offering in-state tuition to those who were in the country without proof of legal residency.[47] The restrictions on immigration, the punishments, the deputizing of local police as immigration agents, and the fortifying of the US-Mexico border are all tactics that the Trump administration employs with vigor today. They had their genesis in the Clinton White House and were amplified after 9/11 and then again in the Trump era, but the blueprint was laid out decades ago. The laws that Clinton signed accelerated a war against immigrants and Mexico. Oddly, there were no laws that acknowledged a need for labor or legal immigrants. As usual, they did not address the root causes of migration—which are, traditionally, poverty and violence in the sending countries. Immigrants continued to come to the United States for better jobs and better lives; it was just harder and more dangerous now. The risks did not slow the pace of migration. They merely made it deadlier.

Doris Meissner, the head of the INS at the time, and the heads of the US Border Patrol, in their Strategic Plan of 1994, agreed that a tightening of border security was only one facet of immigration reform and control. Meissner advocated relaxing restrictions on work visas and a strengthening of family reunification programs in addition to increased border security. Both needed to be addressed. Border Patrol leadership shared in the sentiment that if the border was going to be harder to cross, there must be new approaches to let a workforce migrate more freely—and legally. The Clinton administration approved of a militarized approach to immigration control, but there were no laws reforming the legal methods by which immigrants could come. As a matter of fact, the Clinton administration approved legislation that did the exact opposite. Clinton signed laws that restricted the flow of immigrants as well as their access to services and restricted their rights. Clinton laid the groundwork for where the United States is today—militarizing the border and creating a deadly war against immigrants—and at the same time approving laws that seemed deeply unfriendly to those trying to come or stay legally.

What militarizing the border and signing restrictive immigration laws did in addition to making it more difficult to enter and stay in the United States was to drive immigrants deeper underground and increase organized crime as well as create a massive death toll. In my own reporting, I witnessed numerous immigrants who had been deported attempt to reenter the United States by any means possible because there were no longer any legal means to unite with their families. Instead of migrating back and forth, as had been customary for millions of transient migrants who would come for seasonal work and return to Mexico when the job was done, now they would stay. The new laws created a pressure cooker effect, causing the undocumented population to swell because it became next to impossible to go back and forth. Undocumented immigrants who had successfully made it to the United States would set down roots and then send for their families in Mexico, thereby increasing the illegal migration trade and undocumented population size in the United States. That is, the laws caused the undocumented population in the country to soar because seasonal migration was more difficult and family unification was more important than the penalties.

In all, the policies of the Clinton administration changed the face of immigration in the United States forever. The border became a war zone, and the interior became an inhospitable place for immigrants to live. Probably most insidiously, it

identified the term *immigrant* as negative in ways that allowed
punitive measures, even death, to be overlooked. Going after
immigrants also became locked into the political lexicon. The
fact that these new punitive and seemingly anti-immigrant
measures had first been overseen by a Democratic president
is lost on most. The immigration laws passed during Clinton's
tenure laid the foundation for the Bush era, which saw the
largest border security expansion in US history. The Clinton
era also paved the way for Obama to become the "deporter in
chief" and has allowed the Trump administration to pursue
building an impenetrable wall on the US-Mexico border, deport
immigrants at an unprecedented pace, and separate immigrant
children from their parents. Not only did the Clinton administration lay down the legal framework for more border security
and punitive laws against immigrants, it perpetuated a negative,
anti-immigrant stereotype that remains in the political lexicon
today.

3

The Military Arrives
at the Border

The US military has had a presence at the US-Mexico border since the establishment of that border during the Mexican-American War of 1846, which lasted two years and garnered the United States about a third of Mexico's territory. The newly acquired US territory included Arizona, California, and New Mexico along with parts of Wyoming, Colorado, Nevada, and Utah. The country had acquired the territory of Texas about a decade before. The Treaty of Guadalupe Hidalgo, which both countries signed, was the first step in creating the boundary that is the US-Mexico border today. The US military returned often to patrol the new territory before the creation of the US Border Patrol and also after that to help the Army Corps of Engineers to build border security infrastructure. In addition, border state governors have deployed National Guard troops to assist Border Patrol efforts. In 1989, with the creation of the controversial Joint Task

Force-6, the military acted tactically and like a police force for the first time—with deadly results.

On May 20, 1997, a member of the US military shot and killed eighteen-year-old Esequiel Hernández Jr. in Redford, Texas.

A US citizen and a high school sophomore, he would herd his family's forty goats near the border every afternoon after school. He walked the same path daily past the ruins of a Spanish mission, through an abandoned US Army post, and down to the Rio Grande, where his goats could drink. He had been a popular kid at Presidio High School and the only boy to sign up for the folk dance troupe. His friends had called him Skeetch or Zeke because he was tall and lanky.[1]

Esequiel had loved being a cowboy, wearing an embroidered shirt and white cowboy hat to ride his horse in parades. He had had no plans for college and most likely would have continued to live off the land like his father and most of his family before him. He had thought about becoming a soldier; the US Marines recruiting poster tacked above his bed was a reminder of his dream.

The night he was shot, Esequiel had been on his usual walk near the border, not realizing that his route ran near a drug-smuggling corridor.

Corporal Clemente M. Banuelos had been on patrol at Border Patrol's request as part of a Joint Task Force-6 counter-drug mission.[2] He said later that he had mistaken Esequiel for a drug smuggler, alleging that the boy had fired two shots toward him and the four marines with him. Banuelos had "returned fire," hitting Esequiel under the arm.

Despite evidence suggesting that Esequiel had not fired a weapon, a Texas grand jury decided that there were insufficient grounds for an indictment. Not until twenty years later did the Marine Corps release a report acknowledging that its men had used questionable tactics.

Though the US military has always had a presence at the US-Mexico border, before the death of Esequiel Hernández Jr., it had never had actual missions there. The military had only done training and built border security infrastructure, and the National Guard had stood alongside Border Patrol agents to fortify the border. The US Marines are trained to perceive enemies and eradicate them, not to police civilians. They had not been prepared for interfacing with Hernández, a civilian. Inviting military might into an arena it had not trained for was only asking for the inevitable. Even Esequiel's death, however, was not enough to call into question the military's role at the border.

- - -

I first noticed the military's presence at the border in 1996, on a drive along Monument Road in southern San Diego, near where I grew up. Sometimes I drove there to clear my head or just look at the beautiful scenery, where there were numerous birds of prey, rare water birds, raccoons, foxes, and even the occasional lynx. Every so often, I would park my car and hike along the many trails that crossed through the hills and mesas. One of my favorite pastimes was excavating for fossils. The hills had once been part of an ancient seafloor—you didn't have to look too hard to find proof. Their bare, soft sandstone cliffs yielded a variety of ancient shells and sea creatures embedded among smooth, rounded stones and loose sand.

There, I could actually touch the corrugated metal border fence that had been in place since Operation Gatekeeper. Border Patrol agents parked in the same clearing to survey the area. Their presence never bothered me. I'd walk up and let them know I was going on a hike or to look for ancient shells. The area was public, and horseback riders, bird-watchers, naturalists, and migrants all visited it; as long as I didn't interfere with Border Patrol activity, I had every reason to be there. Agents never even said to me that this area so close to the border was dangerous. Migrants crossed here frequently. To me, it was just a wild patch of land available for exploration.

But on this particular trip, something was different. I pulled onto the dirt road to park there as I had dozens of times before. Instead of a few Border Patrol vehicles, I saw a tan Humvee that looked rather military. As soon as I stopped, someone whom I think was a member of the US military met me. He did not identify himself as military, but he wore camouflage, and his face was painted to match it. He wore a dark-green helmet, and a rifle hung from his shoulder.

The serviceman approached and asked what I was doing there. I told him that I was just going excavating as a hobby. He brusquely said that I had to leave immediately. I asked why, explaining that I lived close by and had been coming to the area for years. He didn't explain; he just said that the area was now off-limits and I had to leave. He stood staring at me, clearly not going to change his mind or tell me why he was there. I had never been turned away from the area, even though it was always full of Border Patrol agents. Something had shifted. Had the US military arrived to police the border?

The answer was not so straightforward. According to the Posse Comitatus Act that President Rutherford B. Hayes signed in 1878, the military cannot be used as a municipal police force or for civilian law enforcement unless the Constitution or an act of Congress authorizes it. The president of the United States is supposed to deploy the military within the bounds of the United States only when he or she believes that civilian law enforcement is not doing its job properly or extraordinary circumstances prohibit it from doing so. Using military personnel to enforce US laws is outside of tradition. It is fraught with obvious problems—the specter of military tactics deployed against a civilian population and of creating a police state.

Under the auspices of the War on Drugs that began in the Nixon administration and continued into the George H. W. Bush administration, the federal government began to chip away at the restrictions in the Posse Comitatus Act and enlarge the scope of military jurisdiction within the boundaries of the

United States. These expansions of power were sometimes referred to as "amendments," as they were added without changes to the wording of the original law.[3] The Obama administration had its hand in similar amendments.

Also, within a 1982 defense bill, Congress allowed the military to loan equipment and facilities to civilian law enforcement agencies. In this case, military personnel still could not directly participate in actions,[4] but a 1989 bill allowed them to work in the field and even issue arrest warrants.[5]

In 1991, the Posse Comitatus Act was amended to authorize the military to conduct armed antidrug operations within the bounds of the country—a task reserved for local police up until then.[6] In 2006, President George W. Bush wanted Congress to amend federal law so that US armed forces could be used to restore public order after a natural disaster or even a terrorist attack.

Congressional defense bills have continued to expand the military's role in the country ever since.[7] In 2005, Congress clarified its own stance on the effect of the Posse Comitatus Act on the use of the military on US soil, amending it with a resolution that states, "by its express terms, the Posse Comitatus Act is not a complete barrier to the use of the Armed Forces for a range of domestic purposes, including law enforcement functions, when the use of the Armed Forces is authorized by Act of Congress or the President determines that the use of the Armed Forces is required to fulfill the President's obligations under the Constitution to respond promptly in time of war, insurrection, or other serious emergency."[8] This, in effect, allows the president to order troops be sent to the US-Mexico border, for example. In 2006, President George W. Bush sent six thousand National Guard troops to help build border security infrastructure in Operation Jump Start. In 2010, Obama ordered 1,200 Guard troops.[9] Trump followed suit in November 2018 with five thousand troops to support Border Patrol efforts to stop a migrant caravan heading from Central America to the US border.

Thanks to these changes in the law, the Department of Defense had been able to bring the military to the US-Mexico Border in 1989 as part of an effort to combat drug traffickers. The Pentagon, headed by Dick Cheney, established Joint Task Force-6 (JTF-6) at the US Army's Fort Bliss base in El Paso, Texas, with the mission "to serve as a planning and coordinating headquarters to provide support from the Defense Department to federal, state, and local law enforcement agencies."[10] In characterizing the nature of the relations involved in this work, Lieutenant General Stotser, an early commander of JTF-6, stated, "Joint Task Force 6's relationship with law enforcement, in my view, is one of total integration."[11] JTF-6 was mainly an administrative and coordinating body for collaboration between the US Border Patrol and other law enforcement agencies to stop drug traffickers. It was originally designed as a temporary operation, but it lasted for over ten years, making it the longest-running task force in US military history. About seventy-two thousand soldiers served in JTF-6.[12]

JTF-6 could not initiate operations on its own. If there was a known drug-smuggling corridor or smuggling activity that the Border Patrol felt it could not handle with its own resources, it issued requests for assistance in the form of assets, personnel, or tactics; these were reviewed, and if something was deemed necessary and legal, JTF-6 would implement it. The strategy was to have the military focus on the drug smugglers, freeing up Border Patrol agents to focus on catching migrants.

Created in 1989 by Secretary of Defense Dick Cheney, JTF-6 also owes its existence to Joint Chiefs of Staff chairman Colin Powell, who envisioned a key role for the military in the Bush administration's National Drug Control Strategy. Others in the military were less enthusiastic about involving soldiers in US antidrug policy and politics. As one Defense Department spokesperson said, "We were ordered to get into the counter-drug policy, and believe me, we were dragged in kicking and screaming. There are a lot of hard, complicated issues to be faced when you're talking about military personnel on U.S. soil. But there was strong pressure for the military to be more involved in the drug fight. For a lot of lawmakers, this is their big political shtick."[13]

The War on Drugs had begun in the Nixon administration in 1971 and had continued into the Reagan administration. Then it was George H. W. Bush's turn to put his stamp on US efforts to curtail the smuggling of illegal narcotics across the US-Mexico border. In 1989, President Bush announced to Congress that America's drug problem had reached epidemic proportions. He suggested that the fight against it "could not be won on any single front alone." The decision to ramp up efforts in the War on Drugs and to include the military had been based primarily on a 1985 study by the National Institute on Drug Abuse, which reported results that were "dramatic and startling." Although overall drug use was down, drug-related crimes were up. The spread of HIV from IV drug users was also on the rise. The report also highlighted the fact that powerful drug cartels— and Mexico itself—had fought off previous efforts to eradicate smuggling routes, and drugs were more readily available: "Drugs are potent, drugs are cheap and drugs are available to almost anyone who wants them."[14] The H. W. Bush administration was determined to get America's drug problem under control by any means necessary. It supported a sweeping bill known as the Anti-Drug Abuse Act of 1988, and among its many provisions, it aimed to create a drug-free America by 1995. Using the military to stop drug smugglers from crossing the border would be part of the effort.

But military presence was hardly necessary for this mission. Over a decade's worth of statistics up to this point had proven that more than 85 percent of all illegal drugs entering the United States had come through ports of entry in vehicles—not on foot. Most came concealed in legitimate cargo containers that had gone uninspected. Nearly 100 percent of heroin, 97 percent of cocaine, and almost 100 percent of methamphetamine and prescription drugs had been carried via sea and land vehicles. Pot was about the only drug the military would be going after, and half of the marijuana at the time of the operation was being grown in the United States. If Congress wanted to stop the flow of drugs into the country in the late nineties, it should have fortified inspections at ports of entry. Back then, three and a half million trucks crossed through US-Mexico ports, and only 25 percent of them were inspected.[15]

Even though its power was limited, the US military could now act at the border. JTF-6 had created a Rapid Support Unit made up of Army Special Forces troops to provide an "immediate response to actionable intelligence," three-quarters of which was ground reconnaissance in 1996.[16] The troops at the border would be governed by the military's rules of engagement; that is, the laws of war would apply within the confines of the United States, allowing the military to engage with a perceived enemy[17]—organized crime syndicates and drug smugglers—in a place where millions of US citizens lived. But it wasn't clear whether the troops were able to differentiate the enemy from US citizens or the economic migrants who crossed the border. The US Marines' rules of engagement with respect to matters of national security require soldiers to try to tamp down threats of violence by using force proportional to the provocation and discouraging escalation.[18]

JTF-6 carried out 1,260 missions between 1990 and 1993, conducting most for the Border Patrol.[19] By 1996, in the San Diego area alone, 4,200 marines and Green Berets (US Army Special Forces) were rotating in small teams through a secret operations base in the region.[20] When I was turned away from my fossil-hunting expedition, I had probably encountered a member of JTF-6, either a Green Beret or a marine.

Even before the Clinton administration began applying the recommendations of Sandia National Laboratories along the border, JTF-6 had been deployed to help with the War on Drugs in the George H. W. Bush years. But they only began to work alongside Border Patrol agents when the US-Mexico border played a more prominent role in drug smuggling and politics. JTF-6 provided law enforcement agencies with crucial support through nineteen types of missions classified into three broad categories: operational, engineering, and general support.[21]

Forms of support ranged from construction projects and the deployment of ground troops for various forms of reconnaissance to the loan of equipment, military training, and intelligence support.[22]

JTF provided engineering support to the US Border Patrol as well as intelligence analysis and military team training for its agents.[23] The military-style training ranged from small-unit tactics, weapons training, interview and interrogation techniques, pyrotechnics, and booby-trapping to reconnaissance operations. Intelligence gathering and processing support included "target selection" and "intelligence preparation of the battlefield."[24] Intelligence support also included threat assessments devised by a military intelligence officer working with the San Diego Border Patrol sector. One section called "Threat Illegal Aliens" recommended new strategies for selecting undocumented immigrants for drug questioning.[25] Migrants could now be interrogated without probable cause and based on the suspicion that, since they were crossing the border, they could be drug smugglers. Women with children crossing the border could be apprehended and interrogated. All migrants being possible enemy targets was becoming a reality.

According to a JTF-6 official, soldiers on Listening Post/ Observation Post (LP/OP) missions had to see someone physically cross the border illegally before relaying information about a suspect to the Border Patrol. Soldiers were not supposed to draw conclusions about what they saw (that is, whether an unauthorized border crosser was a migrant or drug trafficker) or to recommend a course of action to the Border Patrol. Their task was simply to report on what they observed.[26] On LP/OP missions (and in other ground troop deployments near the border), soldiers were armed, and they operated under rules of engagement that allowed them to fire in self-defense. It would be difficult for military personnel not to see the US-Mexico border as a battlefield, since that's what their training supported.

As images of immigrants crawling over fences and storming the border played on loops on televisions across the country and politicians campaigned on being the toughest on the border, in January 1996, the Clinton administration announced that 350 additional military troops would help with immigration enforcement along the border in Arizona and California.[27] JTF-6 coordinated the effort and used troops already working in the area on drug enforcement. This was an administration's first public acknowledgment that the military, not the National Guard, would be used to aid the Border Patrol in immigration enforcement. California and Texas were now the front lines of the new war. What could possibly go wrong?

- - -

Before eighteen-year-old Esequiel Hernández Jr. was shot and killed, JTF-6 marines and army personnel had been involved in eight separate gunfire incidents. In three cases, marines had "returned fire." According to investigations into the shootings, US Marines had determined that shots had been fired in 3.3 percent of all JTF-6 missions.[28]

In February 1997, four months before Hernández was killed, Border Patrol agents Johnny Urias and James De Matteo heard gunshots while patrolling the Rio Grande. A few moments later, a beat-up white truck pulled up with its headlights flashing. It was Hernández. He got the agents' attention, saying, "I didn't know you were back there," and explaining that he'd fired the shots because he'd thought something was attacking his goats. He had decided to carry a .22-caliber rifle recently since wild dogs had killed one of his herd. The agents told him to be careful where he fired the weapon, but they were not too concerned— the boy's rifle dated back to World War I. The agents decided that the incident required no further action; they didn't even file a formal report. So the marines about to patrol the area knew nothing about it.[29]

Esequiel would have been used to seeing agents on patrol. Since 1994, their numbers had grown in the area around Redford, Texas, where he lived. What he and the other residents in the area didn't know was that US Marines were conducting operations nearby. He never knew there were marines hiding in the bushes at a listening post, surveying the border for drug smugglers. Esequiel was never told that armed soldiers in camouflage were hiding out along the path where he herded his goats daily.

In summer 1996, Border Patrol assistant chief David Castañeda had received a threat assessment from informants who had told him that there was a drug-backpacking operation in in an area known as El Polvo near Redford, Texas. Castañeda determined the threat to be moderate. The region around Redford, Texas, was not known as a major smuggling corridor, and there was not a lot of illegal traffic, including by immigrants trying to cross. But there was some seasonal activity. The size of the Border Patrol in the area was light, and a drug-smuggling operation would tax the force that Castañeda had on the ground. This was exactly the kind of scenario that JTF-6 was designed to assist with. Castañeda put in a request for assistance to JTF-6 headquarters in El Paso to beef up his patrols of the area.

Along the border in Texas, the land is a patchwork of private and public properties and the military always had to ask for permission to conduct missions on private land.[30] The marines obtained permission from the El Polvo landowner in question, but he lived a few hundred miles away and could not tell his neighbors that the military hunting down drug smugglers in their backyards would be armed and camouflaged. Even the local sheriff's department did not know. It was a deal struck between the Border Patrol and US Armed Forces. If Esequiel Hernández had known that marines were in the area working undercover, would events have unfolded differently?

The marines arrived on May 14, 1997, to be updated and trained on the mission. Court documents state that they received only three days of training, which was against the typical protocol that dictated at least five days. They were also trained separately, never as an actual unit. They had no interaction with the local community or neighborhood residents before they began their mission. In fact, they were to remain incognito. Since there was evidence that some Redford locals were involved in smuggling operations, blowing the marines' cover could jeopardize the mission.[31]

The marines were told specifically what they could and could not do if they encountered drug smugglers. But they were given no standard operating procedure for interacting with civilians. Staff Sergeant Daren Dewbre instructed the soldiers that the drug gangs they would encounter posed an "organized, sophisticated and dangerous enemy. Your unit may encounter criminal elements engaged in smuggling, illegal weapons, drugs, and the possibility of personal threat. The gangs are extremely dangerous and will also use force." He also told them that other teams working similar missions had taken fire. He used the term "the enemy" when telling the marines to watch for armed lookouts—and that some local townsfolk were aiding and abetting the smugglers. His briefing notes stated, "Redford is not a friendly town."[32]

On May 17, Esequiel got home from school at about four o'clock in the afternoon. He studied his driving test manual for a little while and helped his father unload some hay. Then it was time to walk the goats to the river's edge for a drink. At the same time, four marines were making their way to lookout post Number 3 (also referred to as Hole 3). They were to observe traffic in the area and anything that looked suspicious, such as possible drug running or criminal behavior. The soldiers were to remain concealed and camouflaged during the day.[33]

While herding his goats, Esequiel carried the .22 rifle his grandfather had given him. He passed within eyeshot of the four marines stationed in Hole 3, and Corporal Banuelos notified his fellow soldiers that "we have an armed individual about 200 meters from us . . . herding some goats or something." From that statement, one might assume that the marines knew that Hernández was no drug smuggler. After a minute, Hernández had allegedly fired two shots in the direction of the marines from about 185 yards away. Maybe he thought he had seen a group of dogs. Corporal Torrez crouched in a prone position, and Corporal Banuelos told him to lock and load. Banuelos told his men to stay prone and that "if they saw the man raise the rifle again, to shoot him."[34]

From the kneeling position, Banuelos, a marksman, fired a single shot from his M16A2, striking Hernández beneath his right arm. Autopsy reports reveal that the bullet fragmented into two pieces and made trails through his chest, ripping through the boy's spleen, liver, kidney, aorta, stomach, and diaphragm, as well as other parts of his body. Corporal Torrez recalls Esequiel being struck by the bullet and seeing his "feet go in the air." Nearly forty minutes after claiming they had been fired upon, Border Patrol Agent Urias arrived on the scene. Urias claimed to have detected a faint pulse and radioed for an ambulance, but Hernández was dead.

- - -

The murder of Esequiel Hernández drew national attention to the military's presence at the border. The *New York Times* headline read, "After Marine on Patrol Kills a Teen-Ager, a Texas Border Village Wonders Why."[35] A local schoolteacher, Leonel Ceniceros, said, "It seems crazy to me now that they were even here. When you think about it, these are young marines brought in here from out of state. They've probably been told there are drug dealers all over the place, you're in enemy territory, protect yourself. But the result is, this good young man is dead." Captain Barry Caver of the Texas Rangers remarked, "It just doesn't sound like your typical self-defense case." Enrique R. Madrid, an archeologist who had known Esequiel all his life, said, "I'm telling you, the only way they could have botched this up more was if they shot Mother Teresa. If there was one truly innocent man on the border, it was this young man. And he's the one who got killed."

The district attorney for the 83rd Judicial District of the state of Texas presented the case to a grand jury to determine whether Corporal Banuelos should face criminal charges for the shooting of Hernández. "The Texas Grand Jury returned a 'No-Bill' indicating that it did not find sufficient grounds for an indictment."[36] In all, the investigation took over a year but found no evidence of criminal wrongdoing. The Hernández family received a settlement of $1.9 million from the federal government.

The US military's assessment seemed to suggest that standard military training was not adequate to the task at the US-Mexico border, given possible interactions with civilians. The US Marines' investigation concluded: "Basic Marine Corps combat training skills instills an aggressive spirit while teaching combat skills. More is needed to place young fully armed marines in a domestic environment to perform non-combat duties. Such missions require substantive training to ensure actions appropriate for the operational environment."[37]

The report maintained that Hernández had been the aggressor but also acknowledged that "the relatively brief rules of engagement training, given to the Marines in a classroom environment, proved inadequate to overcome the more practiced combat response to an armed aggressor."[38]

JTF-6 armed missions at the border ceased as a result of the shooting death of Esequiel Hernández Jr., but the task force remained active in border infrastructure buildup and in training US Border Patrol agents. To this day, a robust, if unofficial, link remains between the two forces: it is estimated that 35 percent of today's US Border Patrol agents were once military personnel.[39] Former US military members from theaters of war are heavily recruited into the Border Patrol. US Customs and Border Protection offers special benefits to US veterans. For example, time served in the military may count toward retirement credit in CBP, and such discharged members may continue to receive GI Bill housing allowances. In the decades after 9/11, those who had served in the wars in Iraq and Afghanistan would find jobs with the Border Patrol.

The protocol changes for JTF-6 were a small concession to the backlash after Hernández's killing. In a few years, though, the militarization of the border would escalate even more quickly as the War on Drugs gave way to the post-9/11 War on Terror.

4

September 11

The terror attack on September 11, 2001, was the single most consequential event in the history of US border policy. Not only did the country's response to 9/11 change the landscape of the US-Mexico border; it also accelerated militarization like never before. The US government had been caught unawares. There was a sense, suddenly, that the homeland was now vulnerable to acts of terror from foreign entities, that the threat could come from anywhere, and that all ports of entry were points of weakness that terrorists might be able to exploit.

In response, the George W. Bush administration raced to fortify the US-Mexico border. The budget for the US Border Patrol jumped from $1 billion to $2 billion in the span of five years and now hovers around $4 billion per year. After 9/11, the number of law enforcement personnel along the border doubled from about ten thousand to over twenty thousand agents within five years. Even though the perpetrators of 9/11 never crossed the southern border and there were no known threats of terrorists crossing from Mexico into the United States, politicians—both Republican and Democrat—sanctioned the frenzied pace of militarization there.

For years, the US-Mexico border had been sold to the general public as porous, and politicians had made their careers by pointing fingers at it as a region of lawlessness. Now its porousness wasn't seen as a threat just to the economy and jobs; it was a security liability. Within a matter of months, the Bush administration enacted a flurry of executive orders, and Congress followed suit, redesigning policy and procedure along the border to prevent another terrorist attack. During the aftermath of 9/11, Congressman Silvestre Reyes, a former Border Patrol sector chief for El Paso, was the chairman of the House Intelligence Committee. I met with him in his office in 2006 to talk about the increase in border security between Mexico and the United States. He felt that the federal government was too heavy-handed at fortifying the southern border. He said then, "There was no terrorist threat coming from Mexico and there never has been." He was opposed to building more border walls and doubling the size of the Border Patrol force, both of which Congress was debating at the time. I asked him why the United States was trying to seal the southern border if there was no provable threat of terrorism. He cited racism and ignorance as reasons: "Politicians have used Mexicans and immigrants as scapegoats for so long that they believe there is a real threat so it's not too far to go to turn them into real terrorists." Reyes advocated for a more comprehensive approach to national security interests that included a stronger visa system and a more robust guest workers system so that people could come legally instead of simply adding border infrastructure. His ideas did not go far in Congress. The border was soon more fortified, and more border guards were added.

Before 9/11, the mission of the US Border Patrol had been to secure the borders between inspection stations. After 9/11, the patrol was seen as a national security force. The new mission statement that the US Border Patrol adopted after 9/11 mentioned "preventing terrorists and terrorists weapons, including weapons of mass destruction, from entering the United States."[1] US troops in Afghanistan were fighting on one front in what President George W. Bush had dubbed the War on Terror. At the US-Mexico border, the Border Patrol was now defending another front.

In July 2002, the Office of Homeland Security issued the first National Strategy for Homeland Security and presented the national vision for border and transportation security in the proposed Department of Homeland Security. The new DHS strategy was designed to coordinate federal agencies with local law enforcement as well as international partners to secure America as a homeland. The US-Mexico border was but one area of concern, but for the first time, economic migrants, the vast majority of undocumented immigrants, were now considered a national security threat alongside hardened criminals and terrorists. The new strategy at the US-Mexico border would protect "against the threats posed by terrorists, the implements of terrorism, international organized crime, illegal drugs, illegal migrants, cybercrime, and the destruction or theft of natural resources." It placed all who wished to enter the country without proper documentation on equal footing. The Immigration and Naturalization Service, or INS, which previously had governed all issues of concern with respect to immigration, would now move under the umbrella of the Department of Homeland Security.[2]

The new department would now manage and oversee all immigration-related issues and law enforcement bodies—such as the US Border Patrol and what would become a new interior enforcement agency: Interior Customs Enforcement, or ICE. Governor of Pennsylvania and former US Representative Tom Ridge would become the first secretary of the Department of Homeland Security. DHS's initial budget in 2003 was $31.2 billion. In just two years, it ballooned to $40.2 billion.[3]

In March 2003, the Bureau of Customs and Border Protection (CBP) was established within the Department of Homeland

Security. The US Customs Service's inspection and enforce-ment functions were transferred from the Department of the Treasury to CBP. The immigration inspection and enforcement functions of the US Immigration and Naturalization Service (INS), including the entirety of the US Border Patrol, were also transferred to CBP—creating the largest police force in the United States. It was composed of Customs agents, Bor-der Patrol agents, and immigration inspectors, with a total of sixty thousand employees and a budget of $13.5 billion. ICE would not fall under the same CBP heading but was still con-solidated within DHS. ICE would manage interior enforcement and removal as well as investigations within the Department of Homeland Security. If there were corruption or rogue agents within DHS, DHS would be the investigative body—meaning, in effect, that it would investigate itself. This opaque system lacked any real oversight, leading to a series of blunders and cover-ups over the following fifteen years.

ICE initially was tasked with intelligence gathering and removing hardened aliens from the country, but by 2009, its duties had morphed to include a massive immigrant deten-tion center complex, and it had become a deportation force under the Obama administration. ICE would quickly balloon to twenty thousand employees, with more than four hundred offices across the country and an annual budget of over $6 billion. With immigration matters placed under a government entity that oversaw the security of the nation, immigrants were now seen as threats instead of being welcomed. At the signing ceremony for the creation of ICE, President George W. Bush said, "The continuing threat of terrorism, the threat of mass murder on our own soil, will be met with a unified, effective response." The creation of ICE placed all immigrants, whether entering the United States legally or illegally, in the same cate-gory as possible terrorists.

- - -

As securing the homeland from threats of terrorism proceeded at a frenetic pace, there was an obvious focus on porous borders. Getting a grip on illegal immigration at the Mexico border would be a major goal of the Bush administration, and with the creation of new agencies like DHS, CBP, and ICE, Bush had some powerful tools at his disposal and great bipartisan support with little criticism. In 2005, a Congressional research report highlighted possible border threats. It stated that in 2004, 93 percent of all undocumented immigrants trying to enter the country were from Mexico, and 7 percent were "Other Than Mexican"—coining a designation that is still used today. The report concluded that the apprehension of OTMs had tripled since 9/11, and "the number of people entering the country illegally between ports of entry, and the concomitant proliferation of human and drug smuggling networks, can present risks to national security due to the ever-present threat of terrorism. Terrorists and terrorist organizations could leverage these illicit networks to smuggle a person or weapon of mass destruction into the United States, while the large number of aliens attempting to enter the country illegally could potentially provide cover for the terrorists." The report did not specify that the majority of OTMs were from Central America.

The "ever-present threat" of possible terrorists entering the country, no matter where they came from, along with the possible threat of smuggled weapons of mass destruction, had seeds in the run-up to the war in Iraq. The Bush administration maintained that the war had been waged because Saddam Hussein might have been harboring hidden weapons of mass destruction. This rhetoric and the underlying fear of WMDs even affected the treatment of the US-Mexico border. Even though the CRS report was clear that there was only a potential risk of OTMs smuggling in WMDs, the number of OTMs was suspiciously high enough to cause alarm. Congressional testimony by DHS then-deputy secretary Admiral James Loy in 2004 fueled concerns about immigrants smuggling in WMDs. He stated

that al-Qaeda was considering infiltrating the Southwest border because it believed that "illegal entry is more advantageous
than legal entry for operational security reasons."[4] This threat
was never verified or realized, but even with a potential terrorist
infiltration at the southern border, the move to strengthen its
security infrastructure was on.

In November 2005, President George W. Bush announced
the establishment of the Secure Border Initiative (SBI) under
the stewardship of then-secretary of Homeland Security Michael
Chertoff; CBP was assigned the lead role in implementing SBI.
It called for securing the US-Mexico border with real physical
barriers such as fencing, walls, and vehicle barriers along the
thin stretch of border. Since implementation was difficult, SBI
proposed a technology fix for the vast and varied terrain where
physical barriers could not be built—a "virtual fence." Defense
contractors were courted to carry out the plans.

Democrats and Republicans alike believed that the border
needed to beefed up and that technology would enhance America's ability to protect itself from outside threats of terrorism.
Therefore, the US-Mexico border was being sold as a new front
in the Bush administration's War on Terror.[5] The border was a
new emerging market for defense contractors, who moved in as
if it was a theater of war and began pushing security systems
that had been deployed in Iraq and Afghanistan. After a full and
open best-value competition, DHS awarded Boeing a $1 billion
contract to develop and manage SBI—which would be a vast
surveillance system along the US, Mexican, and Canadian borders. Part of the technology copied what the Israeli Army used
at its borders, and some would be new innovation.[6] The proving
ground for SBI would be the border between Arizona and Mexico, where most of the migrant traffic had shifted to since the
physical barriers had gone up in the late 1990s. There would be
eighteen towers with technology arrays along fifty-three miles.
Some would be close to the border and others a few miles north
of it. Most were placed on public lands; others were close to

neighborhoods, which caused residents to complain to local media that they would be subject to surveillance as well. DHS's response to these complaints was to forge ahead. It was a critical test for the department. If the system worked here, it would be deployed border-wide, including at the line with Canada.

Boeing would implement a system that included detection, identification, and surveillance tools such as unattended ground sensors, radar, and cameras for comprehensive awareness of the surrounding environment. The system was supposed to identify migrants crossing the border as humans, not animals, and pinpoint their location—day or night. Surveillance information would be relayed to agents in their vehicles at the ready with their laptops, and they could respond tactically.

Boeing hired defense subcontractors to help complete the massive undertaking, such as Centech, DRS Technologies, Kollsman, L3 Communication systems, LGS, Perot Systems, Unisys, USIS, and EOD Technology Inc. While Congress and the administration believed that the US-Mexico border had security weaknesses, defense contractor lobbying and contributions to congressional representatives increased significantly over several years; Boeing, Lockheed, and Raytheon led the way.[7] In 2002, defense contractor contributions to politicians totaled over $16 million, and by 2008, just a couple of years after SBI had been fully funded, they rose to over $26 million. Lobbying dollars saw an even sharper rise, totaling $72 million in 2002 and nearly $154 million by 2008.[8]

From the beginning, Boeing's virtual fence was a billion-dollar boondoggle. Persistent technical problems, shoddy testing, and missed deadlines plagued it. The radar information relayed back to agents was too slow. By the time they got it, any possible migrants were long gone. The cameras on the seventy-five-foot antennas had poor resolution and could not pinpoint a target beyond three miles. The southern Arizona desert is a vast, open landscape, so the towers were visible from miles away. All a migrant had to do to avoid detection was to stay away from them. And the field agents' laptops didn't work well even if they did receive detection information.[9]

The Center for International Policy deemed the plan a failure. "Not only did this expedited border security lack a strategy, but it also lacked a foundation of successful experience in high-tech border control. Instead, it has been based more on dreams, hopes and fantasy—and on the widely shared, but faulty, assumption that technology provided by private contractors could meet the challenge of securing the country's nearly 6,000 miles of land borders with remote surveillance systems."[10] The federal government decided to halt the project and not to allow a single, large, private company like Boeing to implement such a system again.

In 2007 and 2008, I traveled to the Sonoran Desert in southern Arizona to document the implementation of SBInet. I could drive up to the border towers and see that each A-frame tower bore a series of sensors pointed in all directions. Atop each structure was a rotating camera that surveyed the landscape. Since the towers were in desert areas without nearby sources of electricity, gas generators powered the cameras. A flimsy chain-link fence protected each tower, and signs warned that tampering with the towers or equipment would result in fines and possible jail time. Still, it seemed almost too easy for anyone to sabotage the million-dollar equipment. There was no one around for miles, and yet this poorly built and barely protected system was meant to keep people from entering the United States.

I shot video for about an hour before a Border Patrol agent drove up and asked what I was doing. I said I was just taking pictures and trying to learn more about the Boeing project. Without prompting, he said, "They're a joke."

"What do you mean?" I asked.

"They don't work," he answered. I asked if I could interview him about details, and he agreed, provided I didn't use his name or specify the location of that tower. He told me that since day one, the system had never really worked. As he saw it, Boeing hadn't taken into account just how hot the desert is and the fact that heat signatures coming off the ground would distort images just like a mirage appearing on hot black pavement. "The cameras can't tell the difference between a squirrel or a person," he explained. They were regularly triggered by animals or wind-blown debris. "There's always something moving or blowing in the desert, and the sand jams [the cameras]." He continued, "They've never worked. All I do is get false readings all day long, and I don't even look at my laptop anymore. All they do is make me chase rabbits in the desert. You should write that Boeing just made a billion dollars off of junk—typical."

In 2010, the Government Accountability Office (GAO) issued a report assessing SBI and SBInet. It was not favorable. By 2010, GAO had concluded that "SBInet would have fewer capabilities than originally planned." The technology was not working or being repaired properly.[11] By the end of 2010, DHS had suspended most of the programs. Boeing could never fix the bugs. No evidence suggests that the billion-dollar investment was ever worth making: there was no real drop-off in apprehensions from 2004 to 2006; they hovered at around a million per year. There was, however, a drop by 2007 of about 150,000, which economists attribute to a weak US economy, not to the effectiveness of border security. Although apprehension rates continued to drop over the next ten years to historic lows in 2016 and 2017, DHS didn't scrap the program altogether until 2018. By that point, $1 billion of the $1.2 billion budget had been spent.

The Bush administration never publicly acknowledged the failures of SBInet, although DHS did agree with GAO findings and tried to fix the technical failures. Bush doubled down on efforts to secure the border but adjusted his methods. In his May 2007 State of the Union address, President Bush said, "To secure our border, we're doubling the size of the Border Patrol, and funding new infrastructure and technology." As an immediate step to support CBP's efforts, Bush announced another initiative: a two-year program called Operation Jump Start. It would enlist the National Guard to assist CBP with fence construction projects, tactical assistance, and military training along the border. This marked the beginning of the largest mobilization of personnel and infrastructure the border had ever seen. The governors of California, Arizona, New Mexico, and Texas signed a memorandum of agreement with the Defense Department to provide up to six thousand National Guard members to assist with border security efforts.[12]

While SBInet was ineffective, the implementation of the Secure Fence Act, which Bush signed into law in October 2006, did physically seal off more of the border. The law, combined with an increase in Border Patrol presence, led directly to a sharp rise in the rate of migrant deaths. Unsurprisingly, it did little to impact the number of migrants trying to cross. A weakening economy helped slow migration more than fences did.

- - -

The Secure Fence Act had been sold as the first piece of a larger immigration reform puzzle. While signing the act into law, Bush said, "I laid out our strategy for immigration reform. Part of that strategy begins with securing the border."[13] Bush suggested that border security would be but the first step in a comprehensive immigration reform package, but that legislation never progressed and hasn't since. Security first seems more likely to be security only.

Plans to build an impenetrable border wall were on the drawing board for the first time in our nation's history. A doubling of border security personnel was imminent, even if it meant relaxing hiring requirements just to find enough recruits.

During the debate on the Senate floor over whether to build close to seven hundred miles of new border fence, the late Arizona senator John McCain spoke eloquently about what migrants face. "If you believe that the only answer to our immigration problem is to build a bigger wall, then I would argue you are not totally aware of the conditions of the human heart." Even though McCain knew that a wall would only funnel migrants into harsh territory, he voted for it anyway. With the threat of possible terrorist infiltration, securing the border was still a good political move. Senators Obama, Clinton, and Feinstein, among other Democrats, voted for it as well.[14]

The law authorized the construction of 350 miles of additional fencing along the US-Mexico border. It also authorized another 299 miles of vehicle barriers, more interior checkpoints, and technology such as more lighting, cameras, satellites, and unmanned drones to complement the infrastructure already in place. Congress appropriated $1.4 billion to construct the barriers, but maintenance estimates for a twenty-five-year period were upward of $50 billion.[15] The new law also doubled the size of the US Border Patrol force. Before 9/11, the patrol numbered close to nine thousand agents, but the Secure Fence Act allowed it to increase to twenty thousand. The budget for border security also more than doubled—from $4.6 billion in 2001 to $10.4 billion in 2007.

After the Secure Fence Act had been in place for a few years, I spoke with Doris Meissner, the former INS commissioner who had approved and signed the Border Patrol Strategic Plan of 1994. She described the border policy of fencing and forcing migration through treacherous terrain as indefensible. Jorge Bustamante, the special rapporteur on migration for the United Nations, was similarly critical. He was clear that the journey was now intentionally more dangerous for migrants. He believed that the country was deliberately using the risk of death or bodily harm as a deterrent to crossings. "They only are not afraid to come," he said, "but actually they are not afraid to die." Even the threat of death would not deter those who had no choice but to leave their homelands.

After the Secure Fence Act, I traveled from San Diego to Brownsville, Texas, from 2007 to 2009 to document the

destruction and reorganization of the landscape to keep economic migrants out. One of my first stops was the desert of
Southern California along the Mexico border. As I've noted,
migrants had long chosen to cross near the city of San Diego,
close to where I grew up, because the climate was more hos-
pitable there. As Operation Gatekeeper took hold, migration
routes had been pushed farther east, toward the mountains and
deserts of Southern California. Migrants began losing their lives
in large numbers as the heat and cold proved formidable. When
the Secure Fence Act began to take effect, the border between
California and Mexico became even more fortified. Almost anywhere you could build a fence, one went up. Fences extended
eastward from the city of San Diego. Very few regions along
the border were open for crossing. Mountainous areas were left
open because it was impossible to build fences there, so that's
where many migrants crossed. The most inhospitable deserts
were left open due to the difficulty of building walls in sand—as
well as the roads to access and maintain them. Migrants crossed
there, too.

Another area left open and without fencing had its own natural, lethal barrier.

The All-American Canal runs for eighty miles along the border in the some of the hottest desert of California. Construction
of the canal was completed in 1942, and it was used to tap water
from the Colorado River and convey it to the rich agricultural
lands of the Imperial Valley of California. For years, migrants
who tried to cross the 250-foot wide canal found that it wasn't
so easy to swim. Its water was cold and swift and twenty-five
feet deep. By the time the barriers called for in the new law
were put in place in 2008 and 2009, the All-American Canal by
some accounts had become the deadliest body of water in the
country.[16]

Migrants could easily drown here. They might take off their
clothes and hold them above their heads to keep them dry as they
tried to swim. Some jumped in with clothes and shoes, the wet

weight of their garments making swimming more difficult. Some used empty gallon milk jugs as floats, but they weren't always effective. They tried inflatable rafts, inner tubes, or logs. Such devices littered the banks of the canal. Weaker swimmers would hold on to fellow migrants to manage the swift current, but even the best swimmers struggled. There was no fence, but there were also no lights. The area was pitch black at night. But migrants would do whatever they could to gain access to the United States, even it meant risking a swim across a dangerous canal.

Weekly, migrant bodies were pulled out and buried in a pauper's grave in a nearby desert cemetery. Evergreen Cemetery in Holtville, California, looks like any other, with its expansive lawns and its trees, headstones, mausoleums, and mourners. The pauper gravesite isn't visible from the entrance; to find it, you have to know exactly where it is—all the way at the back, as far as you can go. The cemetery is surrounded by farmland, and the back area looks like a field waiting to be planted with crops. At first, it doesn't look like part of the cemetery. But on closer inspection, the open land is dotted with clay bricks placed in neat rows. Each brick has a number stamped into it along with a name—if there is one. Most have the stamp "Unidentified." The pauper cemetery is expansive and is filled with more than a thousand unidentified migrant bodies, most plucked out of the canal. The cemetery owner is constantly looking for more space, because the bodies keep coming.

It hasn't been just migrants who drown there, though. The swift waters of the canal do not discriminate. In 2007, Border Patrol Agent Richard Goldstein, age thirty-seven, was on patrol with his service dog, checking for footprints along the canal. Dogs track migrants by scent. No one was there to see the incident, but it appears that Goldstein might have jumped into the water to help the dog and found himself overtaken by the strong current. Goldstein's body was found three miles away from where his patrol car stood, the engine still running. The dog was found sitting by the agent's patrol car, safely out of the water.[17]

I mentioned earlier that John Hunter, brother of Congressman Duncan Hunter (a representative who pushed for more
fencing along the San Diego–Tijuana border) and his wife,
Laura Hunter, put out water for migrants in the Imperial Valley
in Southern California as a direct response to increased border
security after Operation Gatekeeper drove up the death toll in
the 1990s. As I've noted, John felt somewhat responsible for the
deaths since he had helped his brother raise campaign money.
He and his wife also tried to bring attention to the deaths in the
canal, which were also a result of the shift in migration routes.
Before the fences had gone up in San Diego, there were one or
two deaths every year, mostly of locals. But by 1998, there were
over thirty a year.

John and Laura Hunter visited the monthly public board
meeting of the Imperial Irrigation District (IID), the agency
that manages the All-American Canal. The couple would plead
for the board members to add safety features to the canal. John
had year-by-year death statistics; an average of thirty-plus bodies per year were recovered. John always pointed out, "That's
just the ones that are found. Bodies will sink after they've been
floating for a while, and you'll never find them." There were
hundreds more reports of missing persons from the area, and
Mexican officials had claimed to have picked up bodies from
the Mexico side of the canal. John had even drawn up a detailed
PowerPoint presentation of his proposed safety features, back-
ing it up with files, photographs, and data. He did a cost analysis for the board. "I'm a real rocket scientist," he would say.
"I'm a right-wing guy, and I believe in border security, but I
just want to save lives." His wife, Laura, had obtained a black-
bound booklet from the local coroner's office that listed every
body that had been pulled out of the canal in recent decades.
There were hundreds of entries, the vast majority of which were
anonymous. The booklet did contain a few names, countries of
origin, or other identifying information.

The All-American Canal has several elevation drops as it runs its course from the Colorado River to the desert farmland of California. The drops had hydraulic pumps to capture the electricity generated by the running water. Dead bodies would get stuck there, and many were dismembered by the swift current. Most were unidentifiable by the time they were retrieved (if they ever were). At the board meetings, Laura would take the podium and hold the booklet up to the assembly, shaking it with anger and emotion, showing the board with page after page just how many bodies had been pulled from the canal. Each month, she tried to appeal to the members' consciences, and each month, they met her with blank stares.

One IID board member, Stella Mendoza, repeatedly remarked that adding safety features to the canal would only entice migrants to swim it, thinking it was safe. Mendoza thought that the few No Trespassing signs should serve as adequate warning not to enter the canal.

I accompanied John and Laura Hunter on several of their pushes to get the IID board of directors to listen to their pleas. During meetings, John Hunter declared how easy it would be to make the canal safe. Mendoza, who was as defiant and as unconvinced that safety features needed to be added, insisted that people were taking their lives into their own hands and if they happened to drown, it was not really the concern of the IID. She even admitted that people would continue to drown in the canal for years to come.

The news program 60 Minutes covered the story showing one of these meetings. When it aired, the Imperial Irrigation District and its board members, especially Stella Mendoza, came under national fire.[18] She looked cold and heartless against the backdrop of hundreds of drowning deaths. The nation got to see the pauper cemetery where hundreds of unidentified migrant bodies were buried. Stephanie Martinez, a widow of a drowning victim, related her harrowing story of hearing that her husband had drowned in the canal on Valentine's Day. Her testimony seemed to elicit compassion from the television audience, and the IID received hundreds of calls complaining about its heartless approach and urging it to add safety features to the canal.

By the year 2000, the IID had needed a system for retrieving human remains without using divers, who suffered emotional trauma from the brutal reality of pulling dead bodies out every week or so. The IID had designed a mobile crane to do the job. After the broadcast of the 60 *Minutes* episode, the district installed cable lines across the canal in 105 locations, and more than a thousand signs in English and Spanish warned would-be swimmers of the dangerous currents. Haul-out ladders were available about every mile with beacons above them so they could be seen at night. The entire safety project cost $1.1 million.[19]

- - -

In 2008, there was a congressional hearing on the local impacts of the border wall in South Texas. Members of Congress and experts from all walks of life gathered at the University of Texas in Brownsville. There was a heated exchange regarding the fence that was about to be placed in and around the region. Experts discussed environmental, biological, and economic concerns. There were discussions of land use rights and whether the area needed a fence in the first place, since the region was considered relatively safe and few migrants were known to cross there. There was little to no discussion from members of Congress or the panel of experts about what building the fence would do to migration patterns. The border walls constructed nearly ten years prior had forced migration toward dangerous mountains and deserts, and the border wall being discussed at this meeting would force migration northward into wide-open land with some of the highest heat indices in the country. Border walls built here would force migrants to cross deadly terrain again. This phenomenon had been proven over and over, with high death tolls as the evidence. None of the debate, pro or con, addressed the likelihood of a spike in migrant deaths. A large portion of the South Texas border wall was built, and as a result, migrant deaths in the region spiked just as predictably as in the past.

With the advent of Operation Hold the Line, Operation Gatekeeper, and subsequent increased border security post-9/11, the chosen metric for the effectiveness of increased border security was a decrease in the flow of migration. All government numbers extrapolated from apprehension rates are used to estimate how many migrants actually got across the border. Though this accounting system does not measure migration accurately, it is the only method that Border Patrol agents have ever used.

The US Border Patrol chooses to use the term "apprehension" instead of "deportation," so the effectiveness of border security is determined by how many undocumented immigrants are apprehended. There is no known number—only estimates—of how many get through, and there is no accounting for the fact that a larger force of border guards now apprehends more people. Of course apprehension rates go up when there are more personnel. There is also no accounting for apprehensions of the same person. Many migrants make multiple attempts to cross the border, and statistics count only apprehensions, not individuals. Therefore, the rate of apprehensions cannot be a real indicator of effective border security. It has been proven that migration is always in flux and more closely tied to the economic states of the countries people are coming from as well as that of the United States itself. If the US economy is doing well and the Mexico economy is doing poorly, people come. Migration numbers coincide more closely with economic swings than they do with how many border guards the United States has or how many miles of fence are in place. The federal government does not really know if the billions of dollars spent to militarize the border has actually worked—there are no accurate metrics. Migrants are still getting through, and the American demand for cheap labor is still being filled.

The most relevant metric for border security effectiveness that the federal government ignores has been, and continues to be, migrant deaths. In no official report are migrant deaths used to measure border security effectiveness as apprehensions are, nor are they even considered as an unintended consequence or side effect of increased border security. The federal government claims no responsibility for migrant deaths as a result of its policies. There are no federally funded studies of how to mitigate deaths by changing border security protocol in any way. The federal government treats migrant deaths due to security policy simply as if they do not exist—but facts are stubborn things. The Binational Migration Institute at the University of Arizona has stated that US border security policies created what it calls the "funnel effect" in a multiyear study of migrant deaths, migration routes, and border security buildup that has correlated them directly. The institute's report states, "It is indeed the primary structural cause of death of thousands of North American, Central American, and South American unauthorized men, women, and children who have died while trying to enter the U.S. Border fences and border guard deterrence force migration through treacherous terrain. The vast deserts and tall mountains were left open while border towns were blocked off by increased security. In order to avoid detection migrant routes shifted and treks became lethal."[20]

The evidence that our border security causes death can be seen with a simple body count. In the nineties, border walls began rising in Arizona. From 1990 to 2005, the Pima County Medical Examiner's Office (PCMEO) processed 927 unidentified border crosser (UBC) decedents. There were nine deaths in 1990, when there were no walls. The walls caused a twentyfold increase in migrant deaths. The fact that the casualty count had skyrocketed could be tied to the militarization that had taken hold on the US-Mexico border. In 2005, the Pima County Coroner's office examined 201 bodies—just in that one year.[21] During the "pre–funnel effect" years (1990–1999), the PCMEO had handled, on average, approximately fourteen recovered UBC bodies per year. In stark contrast, during the funnel effect years (2000–2005 and beyond), on average, 160 recovered UBC bodies arrived at the PCMEO each year.[22]

I visited the PCMEO in 2007, a year of record migrant deaths. The large stationary refrigerator that housed most migrant remains was full to capacity—dozens and dozens of bodies. The coroner's office had to rent two refrigerated semi-trailers that it kept in the parking lot to hold the overflow of migrant human remains. The bodies were kept on ice until they were processed and, if possible, reunited with family members. Just as in a war zone, bodies were coming in faster than the medical examiners could do their work, so they needed a novel approach to store them. I was able to step into the refrigerated units to see the bodies concealed in body bags tagged with numbers. It was clear that some of the containers had a full set of remains, but others did not seem so full. Maybe they held children or just body parts. The desert is unforgiving, and a corpse will be only bone within days—or wild animals will feast on the bodies. The smell inside the large refrigerator was unlike anything I had ever experienced. It was strong and putrid, and I could not take a breath without filling my lungs with the stench of death. I have never forgotten it. I could hardly believe the racks, like bookcases, that lined the wall from floor to ceiling with bodies waiting to be examined and processed. I couldn't stay inside for too long—not because of the cold but because it was just too difficult to be surrounded by so many deceased individuals. As I left the coroner's office, I realized that my clothes had become permeated with the smell from the chemically treated dead bodies. I couldn't wait to get back to my hotel room and take off my clothes. When I did, I put them all in a plastic bag and found a dumpster and threw them away for good.

- - -

As a result of 9/11, the Bush administration added another weapon to the border security arsenal. In February 2008, the Alien Transfer Exit Program (ATEP) was deployed in the San Diego, Yuma, and El Centro Border Patrol sectors; the program had been extended to the to the rest of the border by the end of 2009, including the El Paso Sector. ATEP is an ongoing program that moves Mexican nationals from one Border Patrol sector to another before deporting them to Mexico. According to CBP, the program was instituted to break up families.[23] Family separation was not a recent phenomenon. The tactic had its roots a decade before the Trump administration deployed it. If a husband, a wife, and their child were going to be deported, the plan was to send the father to Matamoros, Mexico, for example, and the mother and child to Tijuana—separating the family members by two thousand miles. The program did this on purpose, randomly scattering family once across the border. The thinking was that ATEP could break up smuggling rings. For families, reentering the United States would be either difficult or impossible. They would spend most of their time and resources just trying to find each other in Mexico. Not only that; the federal government concealed from each person where the others had been deported, causing even greater strife for the family unit. Women would be deported with their children at all hours without their male partners, sometimes in dangerous towns. Many of them had no money or a place to stay. They had no way to communicate with their spouses and no way to know where they were or how they might ever reunite.

The journey from Central America through Mexico to the United States can be fraught with peril. The journey across the vast deserts of the American Southwest has cost many their lives, and now the deportation process was also punitive and used as another deterrent to migration. At every step, the federal government was determined to inflict pain on those that tried to cross. The strategy of prevention through deterrence implemented in 1994 had accelerated and toughened after 9/11.

Many conceivable means of making life hard for migrants was explored and adopted. Every migrant would feel the sting. The US government thought that this was the best way keep desperate people from reaching for a better life.

As I was documenting the effects of the Secure Fence Act along the border, I happened upon what appeared to be a soup kitchen in Nogales, Mexico. The United States was deporting migrants to this border town at a level of about a hundred per day after being held in US custody. Many of them had been deported without money, their cell phones if they had any, and sometimes their identification. This was done to make them think twice about crossing the border again. Some, men and women alike, had had their shoelaces taken, so even walking became difficult. Some recent arrivals were looking for their spouses who had been placed somewhere else along the border.

Here in Nogales just by the border, an organization called No More Deaths had set up a shelter where the deportees could have a hot meal. Everyone who arrived through that gate could see the shelter, and all were invited. Volunteers tended to basic medical and humanitarian needs. Many of the migrants were in bad shape; they had spent days in the desert trying to get to the interior of the United States, only to be apprehended and detained in a Border Patrol custody facility for a few days. There, they had slept on concrete floors in what was called a *hielera*—an icebox—because the patrol kept the temperature of the holding cells near sixty degrees: another punishment. The detainees were given little food and water—and were sometimes deprived of them. I heard that sometimes, the Border Patrol threw rations of food into the air to watch the migrants dive for it like fish in an aquarium. The agents took medications from the migrants at their arrests, so those with chronic illness would go days without their pills.

I stayed at the No More Deaths border camp regularly to document the condition that migrants were in when they were deported and to hear accounts of how they were treated while in US custody. No More Deaths was then developing a report to document the abuses. It seemed that Border Patrol agents were allowed to abuse migrants—No More Deaths reported that it was encouraged as part of the deterrence policy. The organization's volunteers called it a "culture of cruelty." If border security escalation was like a traditional war, this shelter would be its prisoner-of-war camp. Even though the migrants were now back in Mexico and technically free to leave the camp, they had no resources to do so. Without money, ID, or a way to communicate, there was no place to go. Some were injured and sick. Where would they go? There were no options back home, which is why they had fled it to get here—going back would be futile. The only recourse was to try to cross again and again and again until they made it. They would try and try, regardless of how hard the journey was or how awful arrest and detention was, until they found a job or a home or a safe haven that was better than where they had come from.

At the border camp, I once met a daughter, mother, and grandmother who were preparing to cross. They were there just to rest after traveling up from Guatemala—a trip of over two thousand miles. They had come because there was no work in their hometown, where there were fewer opportunities for women. The grandmother was ailing with cancer, and the mother needed to provide for her as well as to assure a bright future for her young daughter, who looked about fifteen years old. They sat together while the grandmother brushed her granddaughter's hair. I had been watching them for a while and thought that surely, these women must have been recently deported and were on their way home. They could not be thinking about going north, especially by themselves and in the heat of summer. The trip to America was dangerous. I had heard many times that women were targets, and rape was inevitable.

Armed with my expert knowledge, I began talking with the mother. The other two were shy.

I asked what I always did: "Where are you from? Where are you headed? How long have you been traveling?" and so on. But because they were women and also a family unit, I asked a few more specific questions.

When the mother said yes, they were crossing the border, I asked, "Alone, without a guide?" I expected her to say no, but she replied that yes, they were going to cross the desert by themselves. I proceeded ignorantly to share my knowledge of what women face on the journey. I thought that if I told them how dangerous it was, they might change their minds. I had heard so many horror stories and was genuinely concerned for their safety. I went on about how the women should find a guide or join a group or how they needed the protection of men. I quickly realized, though, that it didn't matter what I said. They weren't listening, and they weren't changing their minds. They had made it to the border after months of travel, and they weren't going back—they weren't even going to think about it. I insisted that it wasn't a good idea. Then the mother put me in my place and changed my perspective about migrants and migration forever.

Kindly but powerfully, she said, "We already made all the decisions a long time ago. There is nothing left to decide." She explained that she didn't want to be in the company of men or a guide. She was fleeing an abusive husband. She mentioned the lack of opportunity in Guatemala for her and her daughter. She told me how women are treated in that country: like the possessions of men. She told me about the health care system there and that if she had stayed, there would be no hope for her mother. She told me she had spent many sleepless nights contemplating how to escape her abusive husband, how much she didn't want her daughter to grow up in a country without opportunities, and how she had to help her ailing mother.

She had wrestled with the thought of leaving her hometown, her relatives, her friends, her job, and everything she had ever known. She had never left Guatemala before, much less traveled through Mexico to the United States. She had only one option: to migrate north. She had already made the decision to mobilize—to uproot her family and enter a country illegally through a process in which people die and women get raped— well in advance of my chance meeting with her. Nothing I said could penetrate her conviction to save her family. No danger, no government policy of deterrence, no ignorant journalist trying to tell her about what she might endure was going to sway her mind. She was focused and resolute. She had already weighed all options, and this was the last and only one. In our brief conversation, I grasped migration as I never had before, and I never again imposed what I thought I knew or passed judgment on anyone. I understood that the decision to migrate is heavy and never easy.

I assume that the three women crossed into the desert that night. I never saw them again.

5

Death as Deterrent

While documenting the effects of heightened border security, I saw the signs of migration all around. The reasons people choose to migrate has remained constant; both before and after 9/11, people have fled political unrest, violence, and economic disparity. The reasons for migration have not changed, but the methods of securing the border have become deadlier and more punitive. At one point, seemingly overnight, economic migrants became suspected terrorists who might bomb the United States, and every migrant was treated as like a potential al-Qaeda member. The United States brought the entire force of its military might against meek, poor, and desperate people looking only for jobs and safety. Although some migrants may enter the country to cause harm, the vast majority come to find jobs and the arrest of criminal aliens, those with criminal records, is actually on the decline.[1] The US security response to the issues of migration has not matched the problems that cause it. We have used heavy and mighty force against poor people for being poor. To date, US border security policy has neither solved the problems that prompt people to come nor kept them from looking for refuge here. Instead, border militarization has caused massive loss of life. If border security policy was meant to protect the United States from possible terrorists, it did so with a callous indifference to migrant deaths.

As I documented the effects of the Secure Fence Act in the decade after 9/11, I found myself in the Arizona desert frequently. Not only was it the region that had received the most fencing and technology allocated by the latest legislation, but it was ground zero for migrant deaths—or, at least, the zeal to seal the border had had its deadliest effects here. The Border Patrol divides the state of Arizona into two sectors: the Yuma sector to the east along the California and Arizona border, and the Tucson sector, which covers the rest of the state all the way to the New Mexico border. The Tucson sector contains 262 border miles and is one of the busiest migration sectors in the country. Nearly one-fourth of Border Patrol agents are stationed there.[2] The Tucson sector also has the highest concentration of recovered migrant bodies.[3] It's difficult to quantify migrant deaths, so most organizations that deal with this difficult topic refer to it by the number of recovered bodies. To be clear, this does not necessarily represent all who have died— just those human remains that have been recovered. There are thousands of missing persons reports on loved ones who have vanished on their trek across the border, never to be heard from again. Many are believed to be dead, but their bodies have not been recovered or identified.

According to the Border Patrol, in 1998, there were eleven human remains recovered in the Tucson sector, but by 2010, just a few years after the Secure Fence Act was implemented, there were 251 human remains recovered.[4] It is important to note that these numbers are derived from Border Patrol records but do not represent the full scope of recovered remains. By protocol, US Border Patrol only counts the bodies that it recovers. If local law enforcement, civilians, or even other undocumented immigrants find human remains on their journeys, official federal numbers do not count them. US Border Patrol numbers of human remains are considered official and are what the federal government uses, even though it is clear that they do not accurately represent the total number of remains found in any given year.

By the year 2000, the number of migrants' remains found in the Tucson sector had grown, but the Border Patrol kept its strange process of counting only its own recoveries. The Pima County Coroner's Office (PCCO) in Tucson, Arizona, began trying to accurately count bodies turning up in the region, keeping its own tally. It counted remains that it received, Border Patrol numbers, and local law enforcement and consular office counts. In short, PCCO counted the number of remains in the Tucson sector more comprehensively than the federal government did. In many years, the Border Patrol's counts varied drastically from those of PCCO. For example, in 2001, the Border Patrol counted 80 bodies in the Tucson Sector, while PCCO counted 163—more than double the official federal government tally. In 2006, PCCO counted 237, while the official federal government count for the same region and year was 169.[5] The feds always seemed to undercount.

Migration routes from Mexico that might allow migrants to cross undetected had been shunted to the desert of Arizona. California was quickly being sealed off, and Arizona's vast deserts and mountains, being more difficult to cross, were left wide open. Most of southern Arizona is uninhabited, so migrants could walk for days in the desert without seeing another human being. The area is a patchwork of public land and Indian reservations that are biologically sensitive and culturally significant, so for the Border Patrol to stage a large presence on national parkland or Native American reservations was not good public relations. Here, there was a lighter footprint by border guards, but there was also an understanding that the desert itself would serve as a deadly deterrent.

On a trip to southern Arizona in 2008, I met up with Kathryn Ferguson, who was affiliated with an organization called Samaritans. At the time, its volunteers patrolled the desert where migrants were known to cross, searching for anyone who was lost or in need of humanitarian assistance. Samaritans sought the migrants out because they knew they were losing lives at a high rate. I accompanied Ferguson on one such reconnaissance trip. We met early on a cool Sunday morning in the parking lot of a Tucson church. Ferguson stocked her four-wheel-drive pickup with jugs of water and care packages loaded with snacks sealed away in ziplock baggies. There were crackers, dried fruit, and nuts, all carefully prepared. She also carried bundles of clean socks and first-aid kits. Migrants' feet would sweat so much that their wet socks would become abrasive and caused skin to tear and blister. Dry socks were always welcome. The back of her truck looked like she was going on a camping trip, except with provisions for hundreds of people. She had obviously done this "outreach in the desert" trip numerous times and was prepared for anything she encountered, even with a reporter along. We drove for over an hour into the open desert southwest of Tucson. We entered a maze of firmly packed dirt roads and passed Border Patrol vehicles every fifteen minutes or so. According to Ferguson, this was an active area for migrants, so, of course, Border Patrol was in pursuit, too.

Ferguson was not looking for migrants near the road; they avoided the roads. If they heard a car nearby, they would hide. Instead, she went in their direction on foot. Every few miles, we would get out of the car and walk into the desert with our backpacks loaded down with water, food, and supplies. Ferguson would shout out in Spanish even though we couldn't actually see anyone. She knew they were out there. "Hello!" she would yell at the top of her lungs. "Hello! We are Samaritans; we're here to help. We are your friends! We have food, water, and medicine." Over and over again, she would shout the same words. We would hike for an hour, and again she would offer her humanitarian assistance to any ears listening in the desert. For an entire morning we walked, and she called out offerings of basic sustenance. It seemed surreal, but US policy had forced migrants so deep into the shadows that aid workers had to go looking for them. We never saw any migrants that day, but evidence was all around. We saw fresh tracks in the sand. Ferguson pointed out the difference between migrant tracks and those of Border Patrol agents. Some looked like they had been made with tennis shoes and sandals, and there was even a set of tracks made by migrant shoes that left an imprint in the sand with the word "Mexico," obviously created by the sole of shoes made in Mexico.

The environment was hot and oppressive by 10:00 a.m. Looking at the desert from the road, no one could make out the rocks and thorns among the sand that made any walking more dangerous and difficult. The Sonoran Desert is also not flat. There are gullies, valleys, and hills as well as tall mountains. One is always walking up or down—rarely on flat land. Any brush or trees are full of thorns and offer little relief from the relentless heat. There are bugs everywhere, and they sting or bite or pierce. The Sonoran Desert is better suited to be admired for its beauty from the safety of an air-conditioned vehicle rather than walking, sleeping, and traveling on foot for days. But the desert was the route being offered to migrants to avoid detection, and regardless of how inhospitable it was, they took advantage of it. We drove and hiked and shouted, and the desert was quiet until we came upon someone sitting at the side of a two-lane paved road.

This was not an uncommon sight—a migrant who could not go any farther, stopped at the side of a road to ask for help. He or she had either run out of food and water or was injured or even lost and separated from a group. Migrants haul out to a road so they can be apprehended by Border Patrol and have their lives saved. They know they will be arrested and most likely deported, but they have no choice at that point. Their options are either to succumb to the desert and submit to death or live another day, maybe to try to cross the border sometime in the future or to return home for good.

The man we saw, Mario, had been crossing on foot with a group of sixty other migrants. The group had been traveling during a few nights when a Black Hawk helicopter began to hover low around them. Patrol helicopters use heat sensor technology to spot migrants traveling at night and hover down close to the group with blades whirring in a tactic known as "dusting."[6] The process stirs up loose debris, and it drives migrants out of the safety of a group. They scatter, covering their eyes. Some, in pitch-black darkness, lose contact and quickly get lost. Others are apprehended by agents waiting for them on the ground. Humanitarian groups considering the tactic inhumane have asked border security to stop endangering migrants this way. The Border Patrol has never admitted that dusting is part of apprehension protocol. I have never found the tactic published in any Border Patrol training manual, but I have obtained video evidence of it and have heard a number of migrants, including Mario, refer to it.

Mario had been separated from his group for several days. He was alone and hungry, and the nights had been below freezing. He had no blankets or protection from the elements. He had been planning to eventually get to New York, where he had family and the hope of a job. His brother was working for a parking lot paving company that had a contract with Walmart. He had been told that business was booming, so he could find work as soon as he arrived. He was looking forward to a steady income so he could send money back to his new family. His wife had just given birth to their second child, and he had had a hard time finding enough work at home to feed everyone. He was twenty years old, and he believed he had had no choice but to leave Mexico to find a job. He claimed that he had been near death when we found him. He just couldn't go on any longer, and so he found the closest road and waited to be deported. For me to transport him or even put him in our vehicle would be a felony. Since he was in the country without papers, I could not by law take him anywhere, not even a hospital; otherwise, I could be charged with smuggling. He requested that the US Border Patrol pick him up so he could live. This did happen, and most likely, he was deported back to Mexico to see his family. But if he was like other economic migrants, he would attempt the deadly maze again and again until he got through.

The scenario was a daily occurrence for thousands of migrants risking their lives to feed their families. US border security made sure that the endeavor was as risky and painful as possible and had enshrined this in policy. If death was part of the equation, so be it.

- - -

As the border security screws tightened, crime syndicates began to organize. It was common for migrants to hire a guide, or coyote, to help them cross. Before border security infrastructure efforts had increased, it might have cost a few hundred dollars to cross, and coyotes were usually locally known and had traveled the route before. After the Secure Fence Act, crossing became increasingly difficult and dangerous. Drug cartels, who had run substances across the border for years, knew of safe routes and innovative ways to get their cargo to American destinations. So running or smuggling people made good market sense to them. Why not commoditize humans like drugs and charge a fee? The increase in US border security efforts created just such a market for the cartels, and fees for crossing the border shot up. The system became highly organized and profitable. It is evident that as border security efforts increased, so did the influence of crime syndicates south of the border. By the time the Secure Fence Act's provisions were being implemented, drug cartels were firmly entrenched in the smuggling of humans. By 2010, it could cost a migrant from Mexico about $5,000 to cross; a

Central American could pay as much as $10,000. The price was higher if you were a woman with a child.

The Sinaloa cartel, famous for its kingpin El Chapo, fought for turf along the Arizona and California border, while the notorious Zeta cartel began to run migrants through Texas. There were vicious gang fights and assassinations that determined which group would control the Mexico side of the border. The cartels became so sophisticated that they operated their own surveillance networks to find weaknesses at the border. From my own direct reporting, I found that the cartels possess extensive knowledge of Border Patrol vehicle schedules and patrol routes. Coyotes have often told me that those in their profession pay corrupt Border Patrol agents to look the other way while they guide their migrant groups across the border. As the United States tightened border security, the cartel-run system of human smuggling got smarter and tougher, and migrants were still getting through with the aid of sophisticated smugglers even as the border got harder to cross. I witnessed a coyote with a group of migrants waiting to cross into the United States communicating by phone with a lookout stationed across the border who was watching Border Patrol activity for him.

On a 110-degree day in July 2010, I traveled to Altar in Sonora, Mexico, to meet with a priest I had heard had connections to the Sinaloa cartel. Nestled in the middle of the Sonoran Desert, Altar was a small cattle town but was quickly becoming a popular stop on the migrant route north. Route 2 in Mexico came up from the interior. Migrants could come up from Central America and the interior of Mexico and catch a bus on this route that would take them all the way to Altar, which lies about seventy-five miles south of the border. The town also has a major rail line leading there. Another important factor was that the Sinaloa cartel was already established in the region. A neighboring town, Caborca, was a central hub for the crime syndicate. This is where the planning and staging of drug smuggling would happen. From Caborca, trucks could be loaded up, and drug mules, or migrants, could be paid to carry backpacks full of illegal drugs across the border.

Since the roads, crime element, and infrastructure were already in place, Altar was the perfect place from which to smuggle migrants as well. The journey across this section of the desert had not been popular in the past; it was only becoming one now because of the buildup in border security. The deserts were scorching most of the year, and there were vast open spaces where one could easily get lost and die. That was all good news for the cartel. It developed a highly organized system with trained guides, routes, Border Patrol schedules, surveillance equipment, and paid-off US law enforcement to assure that the migrants would make it successfully across the border.

The system's success rate from here was high. If you didn't want to pay the cartel to help you cross, that was too bad. The cartel had lookouts all along the border in this region. People were checked and rechecked to make sure they had paid the $3,000—the fee at the time—to cross. You simply could no longer cross illegally without paying the cartel. It owned the border—a direct result of US efforts to increase border security. Desperate people will do desperate things, even if it meant doing business with the notorious Sinaloa cartel.

I was able to witness firsthand how the cartel operates—and what it took to cross the border. The aforementioned priest, Father Priscilliano, connected me with Paco, a high-ranking member of the Sinaloa cartel who was also an old high school friend of his. He was a large, muscular man wearing big gold-and-diamond rings on almost every finger. He was dressed impeccably in gray trousers and a white polo shirt. Everything about him was crisp and sharp, even his demeanor. He quickly laid down the rules of how everything was going to be and that I could not deviate from what he was about to tell me to do. He said, "You never put the camera on one of my men. You only film the migrants, only them. If you film any of my men anywhere along this journey, I will kill you." I had no reason to doubt that he would. "I will be watching you on the whole journey, so don't try anything. Is that clear?"

"I promise you—all I want is the migrant story," I said.

"Do you have the cash?"

I told him yes. I handed him a wad of money: three thousand dollars in twenty-dollar bills. Paco counted it three times. Once everything was set, he smiled and wished me luck. He even gave me a hug and strong pat on the back, which only made me nervous. I was off.

Within minutes of the transaction with Paco, I was allowed into a beat-up white passenger van parked in the church square; Christof Putzel, a fellow journalist, would travel with me. The cartel owned and operated the vans, transporting migrants to the border, where they would meet their guides and eventually cross. The van ride cost an additional $220 on top of what I had already paid to Paco. Everything in this town was run by the cartel, and the entire human phenomenon of migration had been commoditized. I estimated that, given what I had spent and how many migrants crossed the border in this region, the cartel was taking in a few million dollars in cash every night.

The passenger van had had all of its bench seats removed, and a metal I beam ran the length down its center, welded to the floor. About fifteen people could pack in. I was placed in the center of the I-beam, with one migrant in front and one behind me. It was about 112 degrees that day, and there was no air-conditioning in the van. The driver was a member of the cartel, and so were two other passengers. They were there to keep an eye on me and my video camera.

Within a mile from the church, the van veered off the paved road onto a poorly constructed dirt road. About half a mile down the dirt road was a Mexico military Humvee with three Mexican soldiers hanging around it. These military men were there to guard the road from outsiders and only let cartel vans and vehicles through. The dirt road was owned and managed by the cartel, and the Mexican military was guarding the road for the mafia. Everyone, it seemed, was in on the action. The van slowed as it approached the military vehicle. One of the soldiers walked up to the van and counted everyone, including me. There was an inaudible exchange with the driver, and then off we went.

It was a grueling four-hour journey to go about seventy miles on roads that should not even be called roads. The van sped as fast as it could along winding, uneven, deeply potholed routes. The van dove, jostled, slammed, braked, and sped throughout the entire journey. We all had to hold on as tight as we could without seat belts—or even seats—being thrown around the hot van like cans rolling on the floorboard of a car. It was painful, aggravating, and abusive. The goal was to get as many migrants to the border in the shortest time possible without being detected. Making the journey comfortable was not part of the business equation. The cartel was moving people as cargo just as it would ship bales of marijuana—pack 'em in and move 'em out.

About two hours into the ride, we pulled over at what appeared to be a ranch house at the side of the road. The van driver got out and lifted its hood to fill the hot radiator with water from a hose. Two young men wearing bandanas over their faces and carrying automatic weapons with bayonets peered into the van and asked everyone to get out. The migrants and I, barely able to walk but happy to stretch our legs, climbed out into the hot desert. Immediately, the men with the covered faces approached me. One pointed a gun at my face as the other walked behind me and I felt the sharp point of his bayonet on my back. Those guns were bigger than the boys holding them. The cartel is notorious for recruiting boys because they are impressionable and the easiest to persuade into acts of violence.

As I stood there with an automatic weapon pointed at me, a third, older man asked me to rewind my video as he watched. That was the only command I got—to rewind the video, all of it. They wanted to see if any of the cartel members appeared on it. If they had, I'm sure they would have killed me on the spot. Since I had no footage of any cartel member, I was free to go. We all piled back into the van, and it headed north.

The next two hours on the road were as awful as the first two—just as rough and just as painful. As we approached our final destination, night began to fall. We drove into a large clearing, where we could see a ranch house off in the distance. The darkness made it difficult to see, but I heard that we were close to the border and would wait here until we met up with our guide. The cartel members led all the migrants from the van, plus us journalists, to what amounted to a cattle pen. There were probably about fifty people scattered across it, waiting to meet their guide. We would all then head off on foot to the border.

I walked toward the large ranch house, a long adobe and stucco structure. All the lights were on. On the roof was a small cluster of satellite dishes and antennas. Several people in the house sat at a long desk full of computer monitors with what appeared to be night vision scenes on their screens. They seemed to be surveying the surrounding area. Next to the house was a helicopter on its pad. This was a sophisticated operation capable of monitoring US law enforcement activity to ensure that migrants crossed the border successfully.

At the time, the cartel charged $11,000 to anyone going to the United States from Central America. Crossing through Mexico was illegal, so the cartel's assurance of safe passage through both Mexico and across the border came at a high price. As the United States has increased border security since then, the fee has gone up. The cartel had made wise investments in such infrastructure as surveillance equipment and helicopters to protect its profits—on any given night, five hundred migrants might be waiting to cross the border from the ranch house clearing.

In addition to the sophisticated setup at the ranch house, there was a converted barn that served as a store where migrants could purchase last-minute items for their long journey. In the middle of nowhere, this migrant shop came complete with a store clerk and plenty of merchandise. There were bottles of water, cans of food, backpacks, bandanas, extra pairs of socks, first-aid kits, hats, shoes, Bibles, and holy cards dedicated to various well-known Latin American saints that migrants kept with them to assure safe passage. Everywhere around me, it was clear, this was about business—and it was lucrative.

I returned to my small group of migrants in the cow pen, and within a few minutes, I was introduced to the man who would serve as our guide across the border and through the Arizona desert to our final destination—the town of Sells on the Tohono O'odham Indian Reservation. Gilberto was his name. There were four of us: Christof; Gilberto, the guide; myself; and Jose, a twenty-two-year-old migrant from Mexico who was the only one going on the journey for reasons of desperation. We would cross the border that night. We headed out on foot.

After several hours at a brisk pace, we stopped for a break. I took off my backpack to find that I was drenched in sweat. I had only two gallons of water (which weighed sixteen pounds), and knew I had to ration it—but I wanted to drink one gallon then and there. Gilberto had binoculars, what appeared to be a satellite phone, and a cell phone. He would stop every half hour or so and survey the area and sometimes place a call. He spoke in very hushed tones because he did not want me to hear his plans or whom he was talking about. He didn't trust me, and the fact that I had a camera made him nervous. What I could hear informed me that Gilberto was communicating with someone who knew the whereabouts of Border Patrol agents on the US side. We would walk for an hour, stop, then walk back in the opposite direction and then stop, and then again. I could hear him say, "Thirty minutes," and then twenty minutes later, he said, "Ten minutes." A few more minutes later, he said, "Five minutes," and five minutes later, a Border Patrol vehicle drove by on the US side. Someone else was watching patrol activity and relaying the information to Gilberto.

As soon as the Border Patrol vehicle was well past us, we were summoned to get up and head for the border line. It seemed like the coast was clear, and we were about to cross over. But as quickly as we had started, Gilberto got back on his phone and made us stop. He turned us around, and we headed away from the border and walked east for hours until sunrise. Apparently, that location had not been a safe place to cross, so we needed to make our attempt somewhere else. We walked in Mexico for twenty-four hours, looking for the right place and the right time to cross based on communications that Gilberto received. Finally, we were ready.

Along the slim barbed-wire fence that marked the US-Mexico border ran a dirt road that the Border Patrol used. The agents would drag a series of tires tied together behind their vehicles to keep the dirt road flat and smooth so that migrant tracks across it would be obvious. Once we got up to the line, we stepped over the fence and quickly ran across the smooth dirt road and into the brush just on the other side. The guide went last, skillfully using a large shrubbery branch to erase all our footprints. That's all we had to do. We had crossed into the United States undetected.

Then we walked for what seemed like hours. Given the daytime heat, we needed to make most of our progress at night, so we moved swiftly then and stopped only to sleep for a few hours at 4:00 a.m.

We walked all day in the sunlight and heat and I never saw law enforcement, vehicles, or any sign of border security. The United States had spent billions securing the border, but the cartel knew exactly where to go and when to avoid detection. Night fell, and with it, finally, we got another rest.

The next morning, I just couldn't continue. I had blisters on my feet. My skin was burned, and my throat was dry. My water had to last me at least the whole day, so I rationed it in sips and only sips, and it was never enough. By 10:00 a.m., sweat was stinging my eyes, and the day appeared to be hotter than the previous scorcher. I took one last sip of what was left of my water, which was hot now, and yelled to the guide that I could not go on. I really couldn't. He asked if I was all right, and I said no, that my body was giving up. He understood. He had seen it many times before and had most likely left people like me behind in the desert to die.

Fortunately, I had a satellite phone and could place a call for a rescue at any time. I told the guide to move ahead and leave me. I assured him that I would not make the call until he and Jose were far away so as not to attract any attention. I made the call, and within a few hours, an air-conditioned vehicle picked me up, and my journey was over. I was sure that if I had stayed in the desert, I would be dead.

It took me a while to decompress from this journey. I didn't quite know what to think about it. I can't really say that I know what the migrant journey is like. I had a satellite phone, a TV production team behind me, and a nice home to return to. I cannot, for one second, truly understand what it must be like to make the decision to leave your home country, your family, and your culture all to go to a country that criminalizes you and forces you to live and work in the shadows. What I do understand is the inhumane maze that the US government has constructed to deter migrants from coming. I also know that the buildup of border security has only created an opportunity for the cartels that the US government professes to fight against. And they have grown and profited from this opportunity—so much so that, with all the technology and billions of dollars the United States can throw at the border, the cartels seem to be one step ahead, helping hundreds of thousands of migrants make this journey every year.

- - -

In the summer of 2007, seventeen-year-old Prudencia made the journey to the United States to join her beloved boyfriend,

Ismael. She had lived in a rural part of Guatemala, where she would always be a farm girl. The villagers wore the brightly embroidered skirts known as *morgas* that are traditional to the region. Prudencia had had few dreams of traveling to foreign countries or striving to get an education to become a professional career woman—that was not the path of a young girl from her village. She thought most about becoming Ismael's wife and raising their children. She wanted to be a mother; she wanted to cook and keep a good home. She thought about the wedding, the home, the kids, and all that a loving family included.

Ismael, at nineteen, knew that if he had stayed in Guatemala, he would have what all his friends and relatives had—a farm job that kept him in poverty. He wanted a different life. He knew that not even an advanced education would get him out of the cycle—there were no other jobs at home but farmwork. He needed to go to America, where so many had gone before him. He had a relative in Sacramento, California. If he could just make it there, then maybe he could establish himself well enough to send for Prudencia, the love of his life. Maybe they could marry in America when he was successful. He wanted to provide for his wife and dreamed about being a good husband—and to give Prudencia what he could not in Guatemala. If he started a family, he wanted to make sure he could support it.

He discussed moving to Sacramento with Prudencia at length, but she was happy in her village and wanted them to make it work there just like all the other families she knew. They didn't have to be rich. But he said he wanted more. He asked her to marry him after he got established in Sacramento, when he would send for her. She relented because she loved him and wanted to be with him no matter what.

Ismael made quick work of the journey. He crossed the desert in Arizona and made it to Sacramento without incident. He had hired a coyote who knew exactly what to do. It cost him $2,000. He had saved about $300 from about a year's farmwork and borrowed the rest from his cousin in Sacramento. He hadn't had the $10,000 it would have cost at the time to hire a coyote from Guatemala all the way to the border, so he crossed Mexico illegally by himself and paid a guide for the rest of the way. He had been surprised at how easy it had seemed. Everything had been well organized, and there were many other migrants traveling that way. All he needed to do was work for a few months to send for Prudencia.

Ismael worked alongside his cousin as an auto mechanic. The future quickly looked bright. He figured that he could save what he needed in five months and planned to hire the same coyote for Prudencia. The men stayed in contact until the time was right. Ismael had even confided in Prudencia just how easy it had been to cross. He told her all about the coyote and the journey. She just had to be patient, and they would be together soon. Prudencia herself even communicated a few times with the coyote about how to prepare for the trip. She was so excited.

She knew how hard Ismael was working, but months seem like an eternity for a seventeen-year-old girl in love. She wanted to be with him now, and she lost what little patience she had. She convinced herself that it would be best to save him the money and time, finding a way to come to Sacramento herself and surprise him. The coyote offered to take her sooner, and Ismael could just owe him the money. It seemed like a great idea.

Prudencia set out as millions of Guatemalan migrants had before her. She had paid close attention to how Ismael had made it through, and she followed his path. Once in the United States, she could find her way to Sacramento. She was young and naive, but her faith in God and love of Ismael would get her through the journey.

She made it to the US-Mexico border without incident, just like Ismael. She had not had contact with him for a few days because she had no way to communicate once she had left the village in Guatemala. But now that she was near Arizona, it would be just a couple of days before she would be in his arms. She couldn't wait.

She crossed the border into the Sonoran desert during a hot summer day, traveling on foot with a small group. She had had her monthly cramping for a few days, but today, the pain was especially bad, and she was bleeding heavily. She was growing weaker and becoming dehydrated. She needed frequent stops to gather her strength and to drink more fluids. She was slowing the group down, but she could not move any faster. Initially, the coyote tried to encourage her to keep up so they could avoid detection. But the smuggling operation had become a business, and if a migrant could not keep up, a coyote had to make a financial decision and not get caught for the sake of the rest of his customers. Prudencia could not keep up no matter how hard she tried. She was just too weak. The coyote told her she was endangering the entire group. Prudencia protested, but the coyote insisted that she stay behind. He left her with a jug of water and told her to rest under a tree, that someone would be by and she could join up with them.

So Prudencia was left alone in a desert she had never been to, under deadly conditions. She had no way to communicate with anyone, and even Ismael had no idea she was on the journey. All she had was a pair of jeans, a T-shirt and sneakers, and a gallon jug of water. It is unclear what happened next. Prudencia did as instructed and remained close to where she had been left behind. It's unknown if she was resting or so dehydrated that she quickly succumbed to the heat and passed out. We have no idea how agonizing the last moments of her life might have been. Her body was recovered near a string of power lines that coyotes and migrants use as markers to navigate by. Prudencia's coyote remembered leaving her near tower number 78. She never moved far from it.

According to forensics, it appears that she succumbed to the elements. There was still some water in her jug, but her body was already in a state of decay, and wild animals had fed upon it.[7]

Ismael worried that he hadn't heard from Prudencia for over a week and contacted her parents. They mentioned her planned surprise, but they hadn't heard from her either. Frantic, he called humanitarian groups in the Arizona desert to see if anyone could look for her. Law enforcement, including the US Border Patrol, does not look for lost migrants or take missing persons reports. These organizations may search for someone they believe to be alive, usually only in response to a distress call with given coordinates. Random searches through vast deserts for lost migrants are not part of Border Patrol procedure. After a few weeks with no sign of Prudencia, Ismael called his coyote. It was only then that he found out that the coyote had left her behind. Volunteers set out to look for Prudencia near the power poles where she had been abandoned and, in short order, found her deceased.

Ismael was devastated when he found out. He felt his life now meant nothing. Everything he had done—leaving Guatemala, crossing the border, coming to the United States, and working—he had done for her. Her death had cheapened his newfound job and country in his eyes. He stayed in Sacramento but said that he now felt aimless and wasn't sure about the future. The volunteers who had found Prudencia agreed to place a cross in the patch of desert where her body had been recovered. It was of some solace for Ismael, but not nearly enough. Thousands of others would experience the same loss he had as migrants took their lives into their own hands trying to traverse land that no human should be forced to cross.

- - -

With the implementation of Operation Gatekeeper and Operation Hold the Line in San Diego and El Paso respectively, migrant deaths were a quantifiable side effect. But for the early years when migration patterns shifted, records of such deaths are not so easy to come by. Border Patrol counts of recovered remains go back only to 1998, when forty-four bodies were recovered in the San Diego sector. Border-wide, 118 bodies were recovered. For 1997, Mexican government officials have records of eighty-nine migrant remains. Before that, almost no records exist, and the Mexican government doesn't use Border Patrol's sectors in its own accounting.

Though evidence suggests that migrant deaths were minimal before border wall and personnel buildups, the US government has never admitted that its policies are the culprit for any deaths. Instead, it blames smugglers for leading people into high-risk areas and has sometimes even positioned itself as a defender of migrants.

A more robust response to the growing death toll that is still used today was Border Patrol Search, Trauma and Rescue, formed in 1998. BORSTAR agents are US Border Patrol specially trained in search, rescue, and trauma. No doubt, they have saved countless lives—but BORSTAR is a responsive force. If a migrant makes a distress call, BORSTAR is well equipped to assist. But there is little effort for prevention. Neither BORSTAR nor Border Patrol has put out water in the desert for migrants; that is handled solely by humanitarian aid organizations.

In 1998, the United States also implemented the Border Safety Initiative (BSI) as a response to migrant deaths, but with no admission that the country's border policy was to blame for the problem. BSI was primarily an education campaign, putting ads in Latin American publications, television, and radio. Prominent celebrities voiced its warning spots about the dangers of crossing the border. The United States actually thought that telling desperate migrants about the perils of the border would deter them from coming.[8] It did not. What happened instead is that US civilians who could not ignore the mounting deaths tried to counter the effects of Border Patrol policy, saving lives while government officials looked the other way.

Mike Wilson, a Tohono O'odham tribal member and former commanding officer for US Special Forces, served time overseeing US efforts during the El Salvador civil war. There, he had felt that the United States employed its usual heavy-handed imperialism. He couldn't bear to watch the Salvadoran population assassinated and forced to flee for American gain—that's how he saw the US involvement. Dismayed, he returned to his Native American roots by moving back to the reservation. He knew he needed to make a difference, and a life of peace and service seemed more agreeable after his military career. He also entered the seminary in the hope of preaching the good word and leaving the world of war and imperialism behind. What he had not expected was that the effects of US imperialism in Central America would reach him again on the reservation.

Mike became a powerful preacher and took a lay position as a pastor at a Presbyterian church in the town of Sells on the reservation. Sells is the largest town there, yet it is very rural. It has one main street with a few commercial outlets, such as a gas station and a grocery store. Sells is also the seat of Tohono O'odham government; tribal leadership quickly notices whatever happens in Sells.

Wilson takes his vocation and ministry quite seriously, understanding the teachings of Jesus to mean that one is supposed to live as Jesus did, emulating his actions. "Jesus is the way-shower," Wilson would say. Regarding how to treat the poor and the foreigner, there was no doubt in Wilson's mind on which example to follow. He frequently quoted Matthew 25; the scripture was clear on how we will all be judged for our treatment of others in the end:

> For I was hungry and you gave me food, I was thirsty and you
> gave me drink, I was a stranger and you welcomed me, I was
> naked and you clothed me, I was sick and you visited me, I
> was in prison and you came to me. Then the righteous will
> answer him, saying, "Lord, when did we see you hungry and

feed you, or thirsty and give you drink? And when did we see you a stranger and welcome you, or naked and clothe you? And when did we see you sick or in prison and visit you?" And the King will answer them, "Truly, I say to you, as you did it to one of the least of these my brothers, you did it to me." (Matt. 25:35–40, ESV)

Mike had a vocation to help those in need. When migrant bodies began piling up on the reservation in the year 2000 and beyond, he noted that they had died due to a lack of water. His vocation and understanding of scripture required him to help; his training compelled him to alleviate suffering regardless of who a person was or his or her background. Mike knew he had to do something to keep migrants from dying on his tribal land, so he sprang into action.[9] The dead were being discovered near sacred sites revered by his people and everywhere else on the reservation. Tribal leaders did not want him to help; nor did his very congregation. Much like the US Border Patrol, the church's board of directors and concerned congregants expressed that if Wilson helped the migrants, he would be aiding—even participating in—criminal behavior. The church members believed that Wilson's water would entice criminals to trespass on the reservation. If there was no humanitarian assistance, they might go elsewhere. Maybe they wouldn't cross the reservation if it were too dangerous—but water would give them hope. The congregants even threatened to terminate Wilson's services as a pastor. But Mike Wilson didn't even think twice about it. He continued to provide humanitarian assistance. Mike told me he lost his post at the church.

Pressure came not only from church leadership; the tribal council followed suit. The reservation's Baboquivari District Council, where most migrant bodies were found and where Wilson was placing gallon jugs of water, passed a resolution prohibiting him from continuing. The tribe's chairman followed with a statement in support of the council: "The Tohono

O'odham are a compassionate people who have historically helped individuals traveling in the region. But illegal immigration and human trafficking through this corridor has resulted in crime, pollution, and has instilled fear in many of our local communities. These communities and Districts have been forced to take action and we support those actions."[10]

I was with Wilson as he was threatened with the loss of his tribal membership and banishment from tribal lands forever if he continued to care for migrants. Tribal police told him he had to take down the water stations and that he was in violation of public safety regulations. He respectfully declined and continued to put out water. He knew that if he were to stop, more people would surely die. He refused any and all attempts by the tribal council to deter him. It never followed through on its threats. Wilson listened to no one but his higher authority and continued his weekly excursions. No one else on the millions of acres of reservation was mitigating migrant deaths. Neither the US nor the tribal government seemed concerned that hundreds of bodies were collected year after year.

Death became a commonplace effect of the War on Terror at the US-Mexico border. The United States built barricade after barricade. Mostly economic migrants, but also refugees fleeing for their lives, were forced to cross into and through treacherous terrain. As I have alleged, this was the plan—but, again, what the United States had not predicted was that desperate people look at risk differently. They weigh one desperate act against another. Desperate people have few options, and migration, in and of itself, is a desperate act. To risk one's life in the desert is sometimes the best option available, and so people take it.

The most recent GAO report on migrant deaths, which was in 2006, acknowledges a more than doubling of them since the 1995–2005 period. Numbers are actually higher than the report suggests. So there is admission that the timing of more border security infrastructure corresponds with a spike in migrant deaths, but there has been no resolution suggesting that border security policy be changed. Instead, the GAO report suggests that the Border Patrol needs a better way to count the human remains: "Border Patrol needs to continue to improve its methods for collecting data in order to accurately record deaths as changes occur in the locations where migrants attempt to cross the border—and consequently where migrants die. Improved data collection would allow the Border Patrol to continue to use the data for making accurate planning and resource allocation decisions."[11] Migrant remains continue to be recovered at higher and higher rates. Even though fewer people are crossing the border than in years past, the rate at which they are dying (or bodies are being recovered) is escalating. The United States may have made some effort to mitigate deaths over the past twenty years with various programs and rescue personnel, but the problem is getting worse.

As I continued to document the effects of increased border security and a deterrence policy that had sent thousands to their deaths, I had not expected to find that the massive death toll would cause further problems far into the future—well after the deadly infrastructure had been in place. What do you do with all the human remains? How do you bury a mass of humanity? If migrants perish, how do you find their loved ones to tell them? Who is responsible? Who pays in coin, and who provides comfort for the millions of tears? If border policy was going to send migrants to their deaths in mass numbers, the logical thing to do was to create a system to deal with the death toll. Although the federal government has acknowledged a shift in migration patterns through harsher terrain and an increase in migrant deaths, it has never taken responsibility or provided a method or resources to deal with the carnage of this war. That job has been left to local governments and concerned citizens.

In the summer of 2013, a team of forensic anthropologists from Baylor University and the University of Indianapolis descended upon Sacred Heart Cemetery, a small graveyard that rural Brooks County ran. Small metal markers with the words "Unknown" or "Skeletal Remains" were scattered through the dusty grass and along the cemetery's access roads. More than three hundred migrants had died in the county during the past five years, and this is where unidentified human remains ended up. For Dr. Lori Baker of Baylor, identifying migrant remains and returning them to grieving families had become a mission. "Nobody cares about dead immigrants," she said. "They're invisible when they're alive, and they're even more invisible when they're dead." For years, she and her students had been conducting exhumations and gathering DNA samples across the border regions of South Texas. But she'd never gone as far inland as Falfurrias, home to a Border Patrol checkpoint some seventy miles north of the Texas-Mexico border. As she had elsewhere, she approached the chief deputy sheriff, Benny Martinez, to offer her services. "Of course the chief was like, 'Yes, we could use all the help we can get, any help you can give us,'" Baker said.[12]

    She knew that the graves might be difficult to locate. "I can tell you that we have yet to find a cemetery that has a map," she noted. "So you can't look at a map and know where human remains are buried. Especially when they're not marked." Migrants were seemingly being buried haphazardly across the border. There were few resources to process so many bodies, and the federal government wasn't helping. Still, even she was surprised by what she found at the cemetery. Digging around a handful of markers, Baker and her team of volunteers expected to find maybe ten bodies. Instead, they exhumed more than fifty in ten days, all presumed to be border crossers from Central America and Mexico. Some had been buried in coffins; others in only body bags. She planned to come back the following summer, too.

    When Baker returned in early June 2014, she brought a larger team to cover more ground. They recovered nearly seventy more human remains. This time, what they found made the evening news. "Mass Graves of Unidentified Migrants Found in South Texas," read a headline in the *Los Angeles Times*. Reports emerged of bodies buried in kitchen trash bags, with as many as five piled on one another in a single grave. One corpse was wrapped in a burlap bag; other remains were found inside a milk crate. Skulls were wedged between coffins, Baker said. The shocking news attracted the attention of elected officials. By month's end, state Senator Juan "Chuy" Hinojosa of McAllen, seventy-five miles to the south, said he would ask the Texas Rangers to investigate. "This is too serious of a wrongdoing," Hinojosa said. "I'm appalled at the number of bodies just left in body bags and, in many instances, more than one body in one bag."

On June 25, 2014, the Texas Rangers launched a preliminary inquiry to determine whether any criminal wrongdoing had occurred in the processing and burial of the unidentified remains. They assigned the job to Lieutenant Corey Lain, an experienced investigator who had recently been honored by the US attorney in Dallas for his exemplary work on a federal attempted murder case. He was to look into any improprieties on the parts of Elizondo Mortuary, which had been tasked with collecting DNA samples, identifying bodies, and storing the remains before burial; Funeraria Del Angel Howard-Williams (Howard-Williams Funeral Services), which had buried the remains and was suspected of improper burial, failure to properly mark remains and gravesites, and overbilling; and Brooks County, which was missing autopsy records. If Lain found evidence of possible lawbreaking, a criminal investigation would ensue.

On June 27, 2014, just two days after he was asked to conduct an inquiry into the mass graves, Lain submitted his report.[13] It was four and a half pages long and relied heavily on an inspection of Howard-Williams, the funeral home, by the Texas Funeral Service Commission, which oversees mortuaries. He found no evidence of overbilling, no evidence of the use of improper burial containers, no evidence of irregularities with the autopsies, and "no evidence to show that human remains were buried in violation of the law." Lain found that DNA samples were being properly collected and as required by law, and though they had not been forwarded as required to a repository at the University of North Texas, that was only because county officials were "unaware of a requirement to do so." Far from insinuating any wrongdoing, Lain noted that Brooks County's top executive, County Judge Raul Ramirez, said that Howard-Williams employees had built wooden caskets and left flowers at gravesites at their own expense. "It is my opinion," Lain wrote, "that sufficient information and evidence does not exist to support the initiation of a formal criminal investigation."

Texas Ranger Major Brian J. Burzynski, an award-winning investigator in his own right, signed off on Lain's findings. And that was that. "Rangers: No Laws Broken in Border Burials," the *Houston Chronicle* reported.[14] Texas law only lightly governs burials and the handling of human remains; in some cases, laws weren't violated—because applicable laws simply don't exist. Lain noted, for example, "There are no statutes prohibiting more than one set of human remains to be buried with another at a government-owned cemetery." None of the forensic or funeral service experts I spoke with could dispute that claim. But a careful review of the practices that Lain was charged with examining reveals that many laws and standard practices were violated in the handling of the unidentified remains. And these violations have made it nearly impossible for grieving families to locate and claim their loved ones. Repeated public-document requests of Brooks County produced only a fraction of what should be retained by law.

One focus of Lain's inquiry was to determine whether any of the burials of unidentified remains had violated Texas law. But his inquiry was cursory. "It is reasonable," he concluded, that someone "could mistakenly remove two sets of partial human remains believing they are one." And he notes that Texas law defines a casket simply as "a container used to hold the remains of a deceased person" and that "there are no Texas statutes that govern the burial proximity, or positioning limitations, in relation to other buried human remains."

The Investigative Fund at the Nation Institute commissioned Baker's team at Baylor University to do a thorough analysis of the 118 sets of human remains they had so far exhumed from Sacred Heart (the University of Indianapolis handled at least thirty other bodies), and they found potentially widespread violations of the law that would make identification almost impossible.[15]

Though Lain didn't note this, Texas Health and Safety Code Title 8 requires human remains buried in a county cemetery to be placed in an impermeable container and buried at least eighteen inches underground; remains in permeable containers must be at least two feet deep. The analysis shows that 51 of the 118 sets of human remains were not buried in coffins. Fourteen of the remains were placed in red biohazard bags and four in what appeared to be grocery store trash bags. Five were covered only in plastic wrap and packing tape. One set of remains was buried in a milk crate, while another was simply wrapped in clothing. It is unlikely that any of these constitute impermeable containers. Yet Lain's report claims that "no evidence exists to show that the funeral home or the mortuary company used improper containers to transport or bury human remains."

Thirteen of the remains were found above the two-foot mark; five of these were at a level shallower than eighteen inches. The two buried in black trash bags had been buried less than twelve inches deep. The cloth-wrapped remains had been buried shallower than two feet. The ones in the plastic milk crate wrapped in a biohazard bag were found twenty-two inches below the surface. (No records exist indicating that Lain sought out burial-depth information; indeed, there is no record of any communication between Lain and members of the exhumation team.)

Though Lain was supposed to examine whether remains were improperly marked, his report never addresses this issue.

"There were many more burials than there were grave markers," Baker had previously told county officials, according to meeting minutes. "Many graves did not have markers, some graves had multiple markers but only one individual and many graves had one marker and multiple individuals in the grave." Baker's exhumation process was hampered by the lack of a plot record; Ramirez confirmed that none exists—a clear violation of Texas Health and Safety Code Section 711.003, which requires a record of each interment be kept, including "the identity of the plot in which the remains are interred."

Lain also neglected to explore compliance with Texas Administrative Code 203.41, Title 22, which requires durable, waterproof identifiers to be placed on individual remains within the casket. Yet 45 of the 118 sets of human remains had no identification tags at all, making it next to impossible to correlate individual remains with a particular police report or death certificate.

Commingling of human remains was common, further complicating family reunification. One grave contained four skulls and a pile of loose bones jumbled together with a white sheet and a feed bag. In eight other cases, a single grave contained two, three, four, or even five separate remains—some buried only in trash bags or plastic wrap. No records obtained from the county sheriff state that four or five migrant remains were ever collected at a single location on the same date—an indication that remains may have been lumped together during burial.[16]

Despite Lain's assertion that "DNA samples from unidentified human remains were being secured," Baker said that none of the remains she exhumed showed the classic cut marks in the long bones that would indicate a DNA sample had been taken; no more than six had any bone cut marks at all. And no samples were ever turned over to the University of North Texas, Baker said.[17]

According to Lain's report, the DNA failures were an innocent mistake: Brooks County officials were unaware until August

2013 that DNA samples were required to be sent to UNT.[18] But in February 2012, as migrant deaths were soaring, volunteer search-and-rescue groups alerted the County that DNA samples were not being collected. One group, the Texas Civil Rights Project, became so concerned that it solicited a legal firm, Vinson and Elkins, to examine Texas legal codes and prepare a legal memo for Brooks County officials. The nineteen-page memo, completed in November 2012, clearly lays out, citing Article 63.056 of the Texas Criminal Code, a legal responsibility on the part of county officials to collect DNA samples and send them to UNT.

NamUs, which UNT manages and the Department of Justice funds, is the definitive national repository for unidentified remains. Law enforcement nationwide uses it to identify missing persons. While NamUs stores every DNA sample it receives, notes Kate Spradley, a biological anthropologist at Texas State University, it typically does not post the DNA results of suspected undocumented immigrants to its public database. Family members who live abroad can check for a missing persons match only by presenting themselves to a US law enforcement official to have a DNA reference sample collected. "The odds of someone from Honduras getting a DNA sample collected by US law enforcement?" Spradley said. "It's not going to happen." She said that thousands of reference samples from Latin America were waiting to be run through the system. NamUs principal investigator Dr. Arthur Eisenberg did not respond to interview requests; he told *The American Prospect* in 2013 that he may not have been contractually allowed to review the DNA of foreign families.

In the year since Lain's inquiry, Texas legislators have passed only one new law to regulate the handling of migrant remains. It makes the death records of unidentified persons public after a year.[19]

The mounting death toll as a direct result of an increasingly intense and punitive deterrence policy has destroyed families and placed never-before-seen burdens on local governments. No one, it seemed, was ready or equipped to receive so many dead bodies, and the federal government provided no financial assistance. Everyone was left to scramble, and citizens were left to deal with what were effectively the consequences of war.

- - -

While I was in Arizona, documenting the effects of the Secure Fence Act and the border security buildup that had come before, someone told me that I needed to visit the home of artist Valerie James, who lived outside the Tucson area in the vast Sonoran Desert and right along migrant routes. The proximity of the border and the culture of the American Southwest clearly influenced her work. She had begun to notice the migrant routes littered with personal items as she walked her dogs in the morning. The trails had been strewn with backpacks, clothes, water bottles, cans of food, sometimes Bibles, and other personal belongings. Without much thought yet about what she would do with the items, she began to collect them and pile them in her garage. She got the idea to create an exhibit on her property of all the items. The exhibit was shocking and powerful. It's easy to talk about the fact that hundreds of thousands of people are crossing the border and trekking through the desert to reach their final destinations; it's quite another to see the things they carry and what they've left behind. James had assembled a time capsule of migration across her backyard much like a set of artifacts that an ancient civilization leaves behind and archaeologists later study.[20]

James's exhibit showed what people on the move carry and what they find important as they leave their homelands in search of a better life. From it, one could tell who was coming and where they were coming from. I could almost sense the individuals through their items so carefully displayed. There were children's items such as baby formula, bottles, diapers, blankets, and even strollers. There were homemade, holster-like papooses that women had used to carry their children on their bodies. This was clear evidence that children were also making the dangerous trek through the desert. Women and children fleeing from violence and poverty in their own countries would have to carry all the provisions for a long journey—for themselves and for their children. On another display table was women's personal items such as high-heeled dress shoes, dressy clothes, makeup, nail polish, hairspray, and other items one might think one wouldn't want the weight of in a backpack on such a hard trek. James explained that some women felt that once they crossed the border, they needed to look presentable in order to find a job. Since there was never enough money to buy new clothes and makeup, they brought those items from home. The simple items revealed the innocence of the migrant and a lack of knowledge of what the journey would entail. Some migrants had had no idea they would be traveling through rocky terrain, so they ditched impractical high heels or other items that only weighed them down. James told me that as the journey got more difficult, migrants would dump everything but survival essentials. I myself had spoken to hundreds of migrant women, and it was true that many of them had been unaware of what they would have to endure to get to the United States.

James's exhibit also included piles of shoes that had been left behind on the desert floor. Migrants would literally wear them out on the harsh terrain. What did the migrants do after they had to abandon their shoes? Did they walk the rest of the way barefoot?

There were stacks and stacks of Bibles, prayers written on cards, images of favorite saints, rosaries, and even religious candles. Maybe those migrants had prayed every night for safe passage and lit candles to help their confidence and to solicit a divine helping hand. There were hundreds of photos of family members—piles of them. Identification cards had also been collected in large numbers. You could tell who had been on the

journey down to their home addresses. James had collected ID
cards by the hundreds on her daily walks. She had assembled
piles of reading glasses and jewelry left on the desert floor. The
display reminded me of the Holocaust museum in Auschwitz,
which showcased items seized from Jews sent to concentration
camps. From these items left behind, it was clear that this was
the journey of a lifetime. Migrants carried not only the items
they needed for survival on the trek but things that would comfort them and give them a sense of home and safety, wherever
they would make their new homes.

6

The Soldiers

The US-Mexico border has never been more militarized—in both personnel and infrastructure. The United States began to militarize the border in the midnineties and ramped up under the Clinton administration, and then after 9/11 yet again at a pace never before seen. The result is that Customs and Border Protection (CBP) is now the largest law enforcement agency in the country with a workforce of sixty thousand. Its budget grows year after year. There is little evidence, however, that the increase in militarization has stemmed the flow of migrants across the border.

As I've noted, the faith-based coalition No More Deaths has been leaving gallon jugs of water near common migration routes in a desperate bid to save migrant lives since 2004. But in May 2012, just as temperatures in the harsh Sonoran Desert climbed above a hundred degrees, the group's volunteers began to notice that its water bottles were being slashed, destroyed, and emptied. With violence from ranchers and vigilantes a constant threat, No More Deaths installed hidden cameras. It found that Border Patrol agents had been destroying the life-saving jugs of water—often gleefully.

Visible on one video are three Border Patrol agents, two men and a woman, walking along a migrant trail and approaching half a dozen gallon jugs of water. The female agent stops in front of the containers and kicks them forcefully down a ravine. The bottles crash against rocks, bursting open. She's smiling. Another agent also smiles, seeming to take real pleasure in the spectacle. He says something under his breath, and the word "tonk" is clearly audible. "Tonk," it turns out, is a bit of derogatory slang that some Border Patrol agents use to refer to undocumented immigrants. One agent told me that it derives from the sound a flashlight makes when you hit someone over the head—*tonk*.

After destroying the entire water supply, the three agents continue along the path.

In response to specific questions about these events, Border Patrol officials replied only with a general email statement to me emphasizing that misconduct would not be tolerated and that agents were trained to treat migrants with dignity and respect.

But the event was not an anomaly. A volunteer with No More Deaths had complained several months earlier to Lisa Reed, community liaison for the Tucson sector's Border Patrol, that agents had been destroying water jugs. Reed responded by email, saying, "I am preparing a memo from the Chief to all the agents directing them to leave water alone." The agents on the video apparently never got the memo—or simply ignored it.

This may seem like a simple story about a few rogue agents with a negative attitude toward migrants and those that advocate for them, but an abusive attitude of disrespect growing within the ranks of CBP seems to be going unchecked. More cases of corruption and mistreatment of migrants, in some cases leading to death, have left CBP with a stained reputation and apparently little political will to change course. The agency's growth accelerated after 9/11, which did not allow enough time or resources to fully vet new recruits or to emphasize oversight and accountability.

In 2012, I met Demetrio, a migrant in his early twenties from Veracruz, Mexico, after the Border Patrol apprehended him. At the time of his capture, he'd been lost in the Arizona desert without food or water for three days. When he had arrived at the Border Patrol custody facility outside Tucson, he told agents that he felt sick and was running a fever. "I asked to see a doctor . . . and they said no," Demetrio said. "One of them said, 'Put him in there and let him die.'" They had shoved him into an overcrowded cell while he vomited blood and felt so faint he could barely stand. And yet, Demetrio said, he was given no food or water for at least six to seven hours.

Demetrio recounted one devastating incident he witnessed while in custody, the details of which another detainee corroborated. He saw a young migrant pulled from their cell for failing to understand an order shouted at him in English. The migrant was then forced to kneel on bottle caps, the sharp parts digging into his knees, with his arms extended. "They forced him to stay like that for more than three hours," Demetrio said. If he lowered his arms from fatigue, agents shouted at him and prodded him to keep them up. Both witnesses say that agents covered surveillance cameras with cracker boxes during the incident—and uncovered them once they returned the young man to his cell.

Border Patrol protocol requires agents to provide detainees with food, drinking water, and emergency medical services, to hold them under humane conditions, and to refrain from making degrading remarks. But all this is rarely honored in practice, say human rights advocates. Over the past twenty-six years, Amnesty International, the ACLU, No More Deaths, and even the United Nations have published reports documenting human rights abuses at the hands of Border Patrol agents. Contrary to its own protocols, Border Patrol agents have been accused of systematically denying food and water to migrants in custody, forcing them into overcrowded cells, stealing their money, confiscating medications, and denying them medical treatment. Migrants have described agents hurling verbal abuse, racial slurs, and curses and inflicting sexual assault and physical violence—even causing death. Eighty-four migrants have died at the hands of Border Patrol agents since 2010.[1] These practices appear to be systemic, amounting to what insiders refer to as a culture of cruelty.[2] The Strategic Plan of 1994 was to make the migrant journey across the border as difficult as possible. Making migrants struggle was all part of a strategy of deterrence. The strategy, cruel by design, is still fully in practice today. According to my sources on the inside of CBP, cruelty is part of the training.

In 2016, a CBP source who requested to remain nameless for fear of firing or retaliation gave me some surveillance footage. Details of abuse or even death incidents from within the ranks of CBP are hard to come by; like most police forces, it has a culture of secrecy and mutual protection. High-ranking officials there make it known that there are to be no snitches.[3] The video seemed to offer evidence of customs agents at the San Ysidro port of entry poisoning a fifteen-year-old Mexican national named Carlos Cruz.[4] It shows two agents questioning Cruz as he carries in what looks like a duffel bag. The agents ask him to place it on a counter in front of them for inspection. There is no sound on the video, so what was said is unknown except for what the agents later testified to investigators. In the video, the agents pull two large plastic bottles holding what appears to be tea or juice from Cruz's bag. Immediately, the agents seem suspicious and try to analyze the contents of the bottles, tilting them to check the liquids' viscosity and looking at labels. One agent opens a bottle and smells the liquid. The agents question Cruz. According to transcripts, he claimed that the bottles contained juice.

The agents did not seem to believe him and gestured at Cruz to sip from a bottle. He obliges and takes two. The agents laugh as if they are toying with him, and a few minutes later, they gesture again for him to sip from the bottles. He does. Within about thirty minutes, Cruz was in cardiac arrest; a few hours later, he was pronounced dead. He had been smuggling crystal methamphetamine in solution—a novel Mexican drug cartel approach. The solution had been so concentrated that it caused Cruz to suffer a massive heart attack. Records prove that Cruz had had no history of drug smuggling; his sister testified that he had been forced to do so under threat from the cartel of his family being murdered. The agents in question were supposed to test the liquid for illegal narcotics if they suspected Cruz was carrying contraband. If it tested positive, protocol dictated that they should remove the liquid from him and arrest him. Nowhere does CBP procedure suggest that agents should force an individual to drink what they suspect is an illegal substance.[5]

The agents were never charged with a crime, and based on records I obtained, they may not even have been reprimanded—although, according to DHS, there was an investigation into Carlos Cruz's death. The agents claimed that the boy had voluntarily drunk the liquid and therefore, the death was ruled an accident. The video seems to prove otherwise. A fifteen-year-old boy was dead, and no one took responsibility for it. Indeed, there has never been a guilty verdict for US Border Patrol agents involved in deaths. Unlike local police forces, which are, at least in theory, answerable to city governments, Customs and Border Patrol agents are under the jurisdiction of the Department of Homeland Security—the same agency that houses CBP—and accountable only to its own investigators. There is no other body that conducts oversight.

Soon after the Border Patrol began to accelerate its hiring to meet its doubling quota, I met an agent who was still on the inside. I cannot divulge his whereabouts or job title, but I can say that he had been on the force well before the hiring push of 2008–2009, and he saw the Border Patrol changing in ways that alarmed him. "Bill"[6] confided in me that agents were being trained to be heavy-handed. Abuse of migrants was becoming commonplace, and he told me it was encouraged as a deterrent. There was no new policy on paper that allowed agents to abuse migrants—it was just understood and unwritten that leaders within the Border Patrol wanted migrants to be treated that way. He said that if you punched a migrant, put on the cuffs a bit too roughly, called them names, deprived them of food, or treated them like the enemy, you would not be reprimanded.

"After 9/11, the gloves came off, and we were trained to see the migrants as possible terrorists," Bill explained. "Our training tactics changed and became more militaristic. We had access to heavier and more weapons. I never saw the migrants' attitude change. All I witnessed was a more brutal approach to doing a job I had done effectively without excessive use of force for years."

After George W. Bush signed the Secure Fence Act into law, a rush to double the size of the US Border Patrol was underway. The bill added funding for a large force, but recruiting proved difficult. So to increase the force quickly, the administration lowered hiring standards and shortened training time requirements. It recruited veterans of the Iraq and Afghanistan wars, creating a more militaristic force than in previous years.[7]

The Border Patrol raised its maximum age limit for new recruits from thirty-seven to forty, with the secondary effect that retirement age also rose—from fifty-seven to sixty. The Border Patrol Council, the labor union representing agents, considered whether these older agents were too old for the rigors of the job.[8] But increasing the recruiting age would attract more of them to meet personnel needs. Agents who passed a Spanish-language proficiency test could shave off thirty days of training.[9] The effect of hiring so many agents so fast is clear from the increase in their arrests for misconduct such as civil rights violations and off-duty crimes like domestic violence. These arrests grew by 44 percent between 2007 and 2012, when there were 336.[10]

The lowered educational requirements during this hiring phase were widely reported. High school diplomas were no longer necessary; a middle school education was enough.[11] The Border Patrol quickly responded to these allegations, stating that this was misinformation and that it had never required high school diplomas and that its policy had not changed. I spoke with former president of the US Border Patrol Council T. J. Bonner in 2017, who had been active during the hiring escalation, and he declared, "Although a Border Patrol agency spokesperson said there has never been an educational requirement, that statement is a lie. Education requirements were indeed lowered." Bonner was also concerned that the patrol had not been making thorough background checks, either. The Border Patrol had been hiring low-risk candidates, he said, when it should have considered only no-risk hires. The current patrol policy was to defer background checks until after agents were hired, and Bonner argued that it wasn't even doing that. A Border Patrol Council report that Bonner signed condemned the deferment of background checks. "This is extremely unwise and could easily allow criminals or even terrorists to infiltrate the Border Patrol,"[12] the report read—the very people, of course, that the patrol was sworn to defend against.

James Tomsheck, who served as assistant commissioner for internal affairs at CBP during the Bush and Obama administrations, said to me in a 2017 interview, "The vast majority of agents execute the mission with high integrity, but the hiring surge has caused personnel problems." Tomsheck also said that he believed that the lower hiring standards and limits on background checks had allowed a criminal and corrupt element to infiltrate the Border Patrol. "If it occurs at a rate that which is not appropriate to properly vet and screen applicants, it is virtually certain to allow highly unsuitable persons to enter the agency who will perpetuate the problem of corruption, misconduct, and excessive use of force."[13]

Training for Border Patrol agents shrank from ninety-one days before the Secure Fence Act hiring boom went into effect to eighty-one days. The passing grade for its entrance exam went down from the 85th percentile to the 70th. Firearms training was also reduced and did not meet national standards. Bill, my Border Patrol Agent source confidant, said that many new recruits did not know how to use a firearm and that military training, which some did have, was improper for agents. He said, "This is not a theater of war, and many of the new military-trained recruits shoot first and ask questions later. They need retraining. It's much harder to get a recruit to unlearn their firearm training than it is to teach a novice how to use a firearm."

I began to report what appeared to be the violent effects of a poorly trained, rookie force starting after the hiring surge of 2007–2009. Not all incidents of agents firing their weapons are made public, so they are difficult to quantify, but incidents of excessive use of force and killings at the hands of Border Patrol were definitely on the rise. Agents were firing their weapons across the border and killing Mexican nationals as they stood in their own country; people were being shot in the back. There were shootings of unarmed individuals, a slew of killings associated with rock throwing, and an increase in the killing of US citizens.[14]

Tomsheck knew that less qualified and poorly trained agents would compromise the very mission of CBP. "I don't think there's any question that if we hire people that are grossly unsuitable for the position and place them in critical, sensitive positions along the southwest border, not only would it not enhance security, it would likely compromise security."[15]

Congress's mandate was for over eighteen thousand agents by 2009, almost doubling the force in two years. This large rookie force was less qualified, less trained, and more militaristic than ever. The Border Patrol's new reputation was of a law enforcement agency gone rogue, with little oversight and almost no accountability. Scenes of it destroying water left for migrants and roughing up detainees in custody were tame compared to the allegations of its brutal killings and abuse that now went seemingly unchecked.

This rookie force was armed with batons, pepper spray, Tasers, rifles, and handguns. It has an array of military technology at its disposal from ground and night sensors to unmanned drones and Black Hawk helicopters. Along with its military weapons, Border Patrol received military training. My informant Bill, a weapons trainer himself, said that he did not get enough time to train recruits or supervise them in the field. Initial weapons training was a mere eight hours. The Border Patrol Council suggested that it should be ten times that amount. Bill admitted that there were agents in the field who probably should not be carrying firearms.

With its agents' insufficient training and little public oversight, perhaps it's no surprise that since 2010, there have been more than eighty documented cases of extreme use of force against unarmed migrants resulting in death.[16] The response to families and advocates of these victims seeking answers has been silence. The cases, some nearly a decade old, remain under investigation, and therefore, the Justice Department is not forthcoming with too many details. Names of involved agents are usually kept secret, and any video of incidents remains inaccessible. I have spent years trying to piece together evidence of Border Patrol agents killing migrants; most comes from sources other than the US government. It denies or ignores information requests, and details remain murky. Even when the government closes cases, they remain sealed. It does not release details or any information that led to its conclusions.

- - -

In 2009, I visited the Kino Border Initiative, a faith-based migrant-care facility in Nogales, Mexico. The volunteers there saw a marked shift in Border Patrol agents' behavior toward

migrants in the years after the Secure Fence Act. No More
Deaths interviewed freshly deported migrants for three years,
publishing its data in the report *Culture of Cruelty*. It concluded, "In our years of documenting abuses committed by the
Border Patrol against detainees and migrants, we have found
that instances of mistreatment and abuse in Border Patrol custody are not aberrational. Rather, they reflect common practice
in an agency that is part of the largest federal law-enforcement
body in the country."[17] The report made clear that abuses at the
hands of the Border Patrol had always occurred, but there had
been a definite increase. Humanitarian aid workers had noticed
a phenomenon that correlated with the increase in the number
of agents—and less qualified and poorly trained ones at that.

Father Sean Carroll, a Jesuit priest, headed the Kino Border Initiative, which houses a migrant shelter, a medical clinic,
and a soup kitchen that feeds up to a hundred people each day.
"Abuses are happening," Carroll said. "It's not every agent. But
institutionally, there are problems. Migrants are being abused
verbally, physically, sexually. And it violates their human dignity." According to Norma Quijada Ibarra, a registered nurse
with the Kino Border Initiative, "Every day, we have someone
that has been abused by the Border Patrol. I just saw a patient
with a fracture detained for a few days. They didn't give him any
food, or medicine for the pain." I was able to personally witness
this man's plight. He did not want to speak to me, but it was
clear he was in severe pain. He could barely walk and found a
stick on the ground that he used as a cane. He had not been
given any walking aids while in detention.

At a nearby care facility known as the Comedor ("Dining
Hall"), I polled a group of about seventy-five migrants, almost
all recent deportees, who had gathered for the 9:00 a.m. meal.
I asked them about abuses I had heard were common, such as
denial of food or water and overcrowded cells. Had they been
physically or verbally abused or denied medical care? At my men-
tion of each type of abuse, more than fifty people raised their

hands. Most had experienced what Border Patrol procedure described as abusive treatment of migrants in custody—clear violations, if the allegations were true.

In just two days of investigating migrant abuse in Border Patrol custody, some young women said that agents had slapped them on the rear while searching them. Other women said that agents had kicked them and called them whores or told them that they smelled worse than dogs. I listened to accounts of men being crammed into cells so overcrowded that no one could sit or lie down. They stood shoulder to shoulder—for three days straight. Several of the men told me that if they complained of overcrowding, the Border Patrol would add more people to the cell. If a migrant complained that a cell was too cold, agents would crank up the air-conditioning; if it was too hot, agents would turn up the heat. Many migrants had their personal belongings confiscated and never returned. As I've mentioned, migrants had been deported to Mexico without their cell phones or backpacks—without even their belts and shoelaces. Three men told me they each had over $100 in cash and Mexican identification documents among their confiscated personal belongings. Agents had destroyed the ID cards, and when the men asked for their money back, the agents said, "It's ours now."

Bill, my informant, said that he had complained about a fellow agent he had witnessed punching a migrant in the face without provocation and under no real threat. He also saw an agent tie a migrant to the side mirror of a patrol vehicle and drive away. The migrant could not keep pace and was dragged alongside the vehicle. He witnessed another agent, whom he had trained, draw his weapon on migrants and threaten loudly to shoot them if they didn't follow his orders. Such an action is expressly against procedure. At these incidents, Bill felt that he was witnessing the "sanctification of abuse and cruelty" and that agents were increasingly abusive. He complained about many other incidents as well, but his commanding officer told him to ignore them all and that the complaints weren't worth the paper they were printed on.

After I heard Bill's story, I contacted Richard A. Barlow, sector chief for the Tucson Border Patrol, for a response to allegations of agent misconduct. He declined an interview for the piece I was writing at the time for Salon.com. Instead, he issued this response:

> Border Patrol agents are required to treat all those they encounter with respect and dignity. This requirement is consistently addressed in training and consistently reinforced throughout an agent's career. On a daily basis, agents make every effort to ensure that people in our custody are given food, water, and medical attention as needed. Mistreatment or agent misconduct will not be tolerated in any way. Any agent within our ranks who does not adhere to the highest standards of conduct will be identified and appropriate disciplinary action will be taken.[18]

Customs and Border Protection in Washington responded to my request for comment in even more general terms: "CBP stresses honor and integrity in every aspect of our mission," an agency spokesperson said by email. "We do not tolerate abuse within our ranks, and . . . we are fully committed to protecting the health, safety and human rights of all individuals with whom we interact." The right policies are evidently in place—if they were only enforced.

In fact, since 2000, the Border Patrol has had an online complaint system in place that anyone could use. Records showed that in 2009, the Border Patrol received sixty-three complaints along the entire border for all of its sectors. But in a single morning in Nogales, by simply polling a group of migrants, I discovered as many instances of abuse as the Border Patrol had recorded in an entire year. The American Immigration Council launched its own study, making a Freedom of Information Act request for actual complaints from CBP, not just the ones published on its website. The council analyzed data from 2012 to 2015. In 95.9 percent of the 1,255 cases in which an outcome was reported, there was no action against the officer or agent accused of misconduct. "No action" was the outcome of many complaints alleging serious misconduct such as running a person over with a vehicle, making physical threats, sexually assaulting a woman in a hospital, and denying medical attention to children.[19] Migrants do not usually file complaints. They are not informed that they can, and the online grievance system is not offered to them while they are in custody. If a migrant wants to complain while in custody, it most likely will be directly to the offending officer. Further, Border Patrol and Customs and Border Protection no longer publish complaint statistics on their websites.

In my years of reporting on the border, I met very few migrants who had filed official complaints. One, the victim of sexual assault at a CBP holding cell in Nogales, Arizona, had a traumatic experience while trying to do so. She had to ask her offender if she could file and was repeatedly harassed not to do so. She ended up dropping the charges.

Border Patrol complaints go to the office for Civil Rights and Civil Liberties, all under the Department of Homeland Security. Many investigations into the complaints are superficial. Investigators may call an accused agent and simply ask if he or she committed the offense.[20] The agent usually denies it, and the case is closed. Rarely do investigators call the victim or the person who has lodged the complaint. The investigations seem to follow a "he said, she said" system, with Border Patrol's word being final. According to the American Immigration Council, Border Patrol and CBP in general regularly overstep their authority. "Not only do alleged abuses occur with regularity, but they rarely result in any serious disciplinary action."[21] There is no oversight committee outside DHS that handles complaints of shoddy investigations within the department.

- - -

With no oversight and their numbers and budget increasing, Border Patrol agents' violent acts continued.

In 2012, someone told me about a video of a cruel death at the hands of Border Patrol and customs agents. A young American girl had spent the day in Tijuana, Mexico, as a tourist. On her way back into the United States, she witnessed the brutal beating of Anastasio Hernandez Rojas at sunset. She recorded the incident on her cell phone and put it away for a year, not knowing what to do with it. She hadn't wanted to bring attention to herself. But I tracked her down and eventually convinced her to come forward on television.

Border Patrol agents killed Anastasio Hernandez Rojas in 2010. The agents involved had enjoyed impunity until the broadcast of the video on PBS's *Need to Know* in April 2012. It showed the agents beating Hernandez and shooting him with a stun gun while he was handcuffed and prone on the ground.

Hernandez, an undocumented immigrant, was then forty-two but had come to the United States at the age of sixteen. His is just one example of how law enforcement agencies use deadly force without repercussion. I learned of his case while researching and reporting a television segment about the Border Patrol and its use of excessive force. Hernandez had lived and worked in San Diego for more than twenty-five years, raising his five US-born children. It was in May 2010, in the process of being deported for being undocumented, that Hernandez was severely beaten, shocked with a Taser, and killed. The video reveals that at the time, he was surrounded by about twelve border officials.

One witness on the Mexico side of the border said that the agents hit Hernandez with their batons over and over while others punched and kicked him. A Border Patrol supervisor arrived on the scene, but instead of intervening, he permitted the agents to continue. Another official yelled at the officers to clear away from Hernandez's body before shooting him with a

Taser. Before he fired, the agent yelled, "Quit resisting!" despite the fact that Hernandez lay handcuffed on the ground.

The command was likely intended for the ears of the gathering crowd of witnesses. In the video, you can hear Hernandez cry, *"Ayudame, por favor, ayudame!"* (Help me, please, help me). People began to shout at the officers, asking them to stop. At one point, an officer tied Hernandez's ankles before the beating continued. All told, witnesses say, the attack lasted nearly thirty minutes. The same witnesses told me that Hernandez offered little or no resistance. One said she felt like she was watching someone being murdered—an impression later confirmed by the San Diego coroner's office, which classified the death as a homicide. As a result of the brutal beating, Hernandez suffered a heart attack. An autopsy also revealed several loose teeth; bruising to his chest, stomach, hips, knees, back, lips, head, and eyelids; five broken ribs; and a damaged spine.[22]

- - -

Until moments before US Border Patrol agents shot him dead on the night of October 10, 2012, Jose Antonio Elena Rodriguez had passed a pleasant evening in his hometown of Nogales, Mexico. He had visited his girlfriend, Luz, and watched television with her family; at around eleven o'clock, he asked Luz if she wanted to join him in his nightly routine of grabbing a hot dog at the convenience store where his brother worked. When she declined, he set out alone on the five-minute walk down International Avenue.

At about the same time, right across the border, a Nogales, Arizona, police officer named Quinardo Garcia responded to a call about "suspicious subjects" running south toward the fourteen-foot wall that divides the two towns. At 11:19 p.m., Border Patrol agents, including K-9 Officer John Zuniga, arrived as backup.

"I passed Officer Garcia's patrol vehicle and I saw two male subjects climbing the international fence and were trying to get over to the country of Mexico," Zuniga wrote in his report. The two Mexican men were carrying large backpacks, according to the police report. Garcia and Zuniga stated that they presumed the packs contained illegal narcotics and that the two men were trying to evade capture. "I then heard several rocks start hitting the ground and I looked up and I could see the rocks flying through the air," Zuniga's account continues. "As I tried to get cover between a brick wall and small dirt hill, I heard an agent say, 'Hey your canine's been hit! Your canine's been hit!'"

Border Patrol agents responded by opening fire across the border into the dark streets of Nogales, Mexico. Border Patrol agent Lonnie Swartz, a thirty-six-year-old agent who had joined the Border Patrol when he was nineteen, unloaded his weapon, firing thirteen rounds into Mexico. No agents or officers had claimed that rocks had struck them—they had hit only the dog. By the time the agents were done firing, Jose Antonio had received two bullets to the back of the head; at least six more bullets entered the back of his body after he fell to the ground. Bullet marks littered the buildings in Mexico, making it look as if someone had fired dozens of rounds. Jose Antonio had landed facedown on the sidewalk and died there, outside a small clinic whose sign read *Emergencias Medicas*. He had been unarmed.[23]

Fatal shootings by Border Patrol agents were once a rarity. There are records of only a handful before 2009. Even rarer were incidents of Border Patrol agents shooting Mexicans on their own side of the border. A former Clinton administration official who worked on border security issues in the 1990s said that he couldn't recall a single cross-border shooting during his tenure: "Agents would go out of their way not to harm anyone and certainly not shoot across the border." From my own reporting, since the US Border Patrol force doubled and hiring standards worsened, Border Patrol agents have shot across the border at least ten times, killing a total of six Mexicans on Mexican soil.

A disturbing pattern of excessive use of force has emerged. When I first began to notice this spate of cross-border shootings, I assumed that at least some victims had been drug traffickers or human smugglers trying to elude capture. But background checks revealed that only one out of ten had a criminal record. As I dug deeper, it turned out that most of the victims weren't even migrants but simply residents of Mexican border towns—like Jose Antonio—who had either done something that looked suspicious to an agent or were just nearby when border agents fired at someone else. These victims had not even been trying to cross the border. In one case, agents killed a thirty-year-old father of four while he was collecting firewood along the banks of the Rio Grande. In another, they shot a fifteen-year-old while he was watching a Border Patrol agent apprehend a migrant. In yet another, agents shot a thirty-six-year-old man while he was having a picnic to celebrate his daughters' birthdays.

An international agreement with Mexican law enforcement officials states that US Border Patrol agents are barred from firing their weapons into Mexico from the United States under any circumstances. Instead, they are supposed to call Mexican authorities if they witness an incident on the Mexican side of the border.

Specifically, agents are supposed to notify the Center for Investigation and National Security in Mexico City as well as the local Mexican police closest to the incident. The protocol specifically states that Mexicans throwing rocks or drawing weapons are "time sensitive" offenses and "requir[e] immediate response from the Mexican government." Once Mexican officials have been notified, protocol directs US agents to "vector responding agencies to the area of the incident."[24]

As the case of Jose Antonio and those of other victims of cross-border shootings illustrate, however, such niceties often exist only on paper. The Nogales, Mexico, police report indicates that Customs and Border Protection did not notify Mexican authorities when its members saw two men trying to climb the border fence back into Mexico, nor did they report that someone was throwing rocks at US agents.

Of the ten incidents of cross-border shootings that I have uncovered, Border Patrol agents claimed in all but two cases that they had fired their weapons in response to rocks being thrown. Of the six that resulted in fatalities, all but one involved alleged rock throwing. Border Patrol agents consider thrown rocks lethal force even though no rock has ever killed an agent.

Already, the Border Patrol's killing of Mexicans on their own soil has complicated and compromised US diplomacy. In June 2011, Border Patrol agents shot another Mexican national, Alfredo Yañez, claiming that he had been throwing rocks and a nail-studded post from the Mexican side of the border. In response, then Mexican president Felipe Calderon's office condemned the killing publicly and, in a meeting with Secretary Clinton, demanded that US authorities swiftly investigate the "use of firearms to repel an attack with stones."[25]

Sixty organizations, including the ACLU, Amnesty International, and Catholic Charities, responded in kind to the Yañez killing, signing a joint letter to Congress asking for an investigation and calling for an immediate end to the Border Patrol practice of shooting at rock throwers. "Deadly force should always be an action of last resort, and only used if an imminent risk of death is present and no other tools exist to ameliorate a dangerous situation," reads the letter. "To shoot stone throwers is exceptionally disproportionate and inhumane."[26] To date, Border Patrol agents are free to shoot rock throwers. I could find no municipal police force in the United States that employs such a policy.

CBP officials have repeatedly declined to answer my questions about any of these specific incidents. The agency has instead issued statements like this one in response to my questions about individuals killed because of allegedly throwing rocks:

> U.S. Customs and Border Protection (CBP) respects the
> sovereignty of the country of Mexico and its territorial integ-
> rity. Without the express authorization of the Mexican gov-
> ernment, CBP personnel are not authorized to physically
> cross the international boundary when conducting oper-
> ations. Regarding the use of firearms on the border, CBP law
> enforcement personnel are trained, required to comply with
> and be thoroughly familiar with all aspects of the use of force
> and firearms guidelines.[27]

Nothing directly said about firing weapons into Mexico and no
acknowledgement of such.

One former CBP commissioner, W. Ralph Basham, who
served from 2006 to 2009, briefly spoke with me when I was
reporting on a Border Patrol killing on the US side of the border. "I'm certainly sympathetic to those individuals who lose
their life as the result of some of these activities," he said, but
he added, "These agents have to be able to protect themselves
when they feel like their life is being threatened, or the life of
other officers." Still, a 2010 Associated Press investigation found
that border agents are assaulted at a dramatically lower rate
than police officers (3 percent compared with 11 percent)—and
with far less serious weapons, such as rocks or knives, rather
than firearms.[28]

According to a 2004 CBP use-of-force document, "Verbal
warning to submit to authority shall be given prior to use of
deadly force if feasible, and if to do so would not increase the
danger to the officer of others."[29] Yet in the nine other cross-
border shootings I have uncovered, I have found no evidence
of anyone giving verbal warnings before agents opened fire into
Mexico. In fact, none of the agents involved have even publicly
claimed that they issued such warnings. Customs and Border
Protection also protects details of agent shootings from public
scrutiny. If an investigation is undertaken internally, it is not

made public. If an agent is disciplined, that is not made public either. If CBP refers a case to the Justice Department for
a potential criminal investigation, that, too, is kept from the
public.

Convictions are on the public record, but they are exceed-
ingly rare. The last one I could find was that of Ignacio Ramos
and Jose Compean, two Border Patrol agents who were tried
and convicted for shooting an unarmed, fleeing drug smuggler
in the buttocks in 2005. The Bush administration ended up
commuting their sentences in the face of public pressure, and
both former agents are now free. Since then, no agents have
even been disciplined for misuse of their firearms—at least so
far as the public can know, since CBP refuses to disclose data
on either the number of shootings by officers or the number of
related disciplinary actions.

In the history of the US Border Patrol, only one agent has
been indicted for murder, even though since 2003, almost one
hundred people have lost their lives at the hands of Customs and
Border Protection.[30] As noted, in 2012, Lonnie Swartz unloaded
his firearm and shot across the border into Nogales, Mexico,
striking Jose Antonio, fifteen, mostly in the back. Rodriguez had
allegedly been throwing rocks, which was disproven by surveillance video. And he was unarmed. Most of the bullets struck
the boy after he lay flat on the ground after initially being shot in
the head. He posed no lethal threat; the Border Patrol agent had
never been in mortal danger. Swartz claimed that he opened
fire because he had heard that rocks had hit a police service
dog. Swartz was acquitted of all charges in November 2018 and
remains the first agent ever to be brought up on such charges.
I have spoken to members of the Department of Justice, who
have said off the record that it is never a good time to prosecute
a Border Patrol agent and never politically expedient. Charges
are rarely filed and many motions to stall and suppress evidence
are granted, making the prosecution of agents next to impossible. Keeping complaints and investigations at a minimum, my

confidant Bill the Border Patrol agent says, is part of the culture. It's a good old boy society, and you don't rat out your buddies.

- - -

The poor treatment of migrants continues to this day. This kind of response to immigrants from south of the border has its roots in the deterrence policy instituted in the midnineties—making the journey for undocumented immigrants as difficult as possible so that they'll think twice about coming. This was later enhanced with a doubling of the US Border Patrol in which agents were poorly trained and vetted, allowing a culture of cruelty to develop unchecked. The Trump administration has since sanctioned much of the inhumane treatment I discuss here.

In 2018, Americans were shocked and enraged at the crises of family separation, the ill treatment of children, and seeming callous disregard for migrant families, some of whom were seeking asylum. These forms of abuse were not new, however. While I researched and investigated such abuses, the ACLU allowed me access to hundreds of its files on allegations of child abuse at the hands of Border Patrol. Between 2010 and 2015, minors from Mexico and Central America had lodged hundreds of formal complaints detailing border agent mistreatment of them. Most had been dismissed without any serious investigation.[31]

Jaliveel Ocampo is one of hundreds of young people to file such a formal complaint. She says that border agents threatened her with sexual abuse while she was in custody, part of what the ACLU says is a pattern of misconduct by Customs and Border Protection officials aimed at minors that has largely gone unnoticed and unpunished. Ocampo said that an agent in a blue jacket ordered her to enter a cell, slapped her twice on the buttocks, and then said that if she didn't sign her deportation orders, he would rape her. "It's really a horror show," said Mitra Ebadolahi, an attorney for the ACLU's border program, who has been investigating these complaints. "It's a story of egregious abuse of children who are vulnerable."[32]

In December 2014, the ACLU requested the full investigative files on minors' complaints "in order to shed light on longstanding allegations of abusive treatment of children by Border Patrol." A year after filing suit, the ACLU began to receive thousands of pages of documents from the case files of 408 complaints from early 2009 through mid-2015, which Ebadolahi shared with me. Hundreds of the allegations appeared to constitute clear violations of Border Patrol protocols:

- 13 allegations of sexual harassment or assault, including allegations of agents groping minors' thighs or genitals or making sexual remarks and threats
- 97 allegations of physical abuse, including allegations of Border Patrol agents punching, kicking, and intentionally running over minors during apprehension
- 61 allegations of verbal abuse, including allegations of derogatory, racist, and misogynist comments
- 201 allegations of poor conditions such as cold temperatures, provision of spoiled food, and failure to provide potable water
- 98 records indicating that detainees were held for longer than 72 hours

An analysis of the complaints showed that Customs and Border Protection investigations had been cursory at best.[33] Only 2 percent of the investigative files indicate that the complainant was interviewed. Only 4 percent of case files indicated that the accused agents were interviewed. Only a single investigative file indicated that physical evidence had been collected. Only one file noted that investigators made a site visit. No files indicate the reprimand or dismissal of any agent as a result of a complaint. "It's an agency that seems to believe that it's above the law," Ebadolahi said. "Not a single [case] has been prosecuted."[34]

- - -

The Secure Fence Act of 2006 indeed changed the physical face of the border, and the doubling of the Border Patrol
force changed the way that policing occurred with respect to
migrants. After 9/11, the border became an even more dangerous place to cross. Border agents operated with less impunity
as their numbers doubled. It was as if the United States had
placed its military forces at the border, where it would engage
with the enemy without any concern for civil rights. The new
rules of engagement now deemed migrants and asylum seekers
terrorists, so if they were roughed up or even killed, no one
needed to investigate. This was a front in the War on Terror, and
migrants were the new face of the enemy. Protecting American
sovereignty at any cost became the single rule. I have amassed
tens of thousands of documents, hours of video evidence, and
hundreds of interviews that show that the violation of basic
human rights was prevalent. Nothing I have reported so far has
led to the arrest and conviction of those responsible.

7

The War at the Border Expands

In 2014, while working on a documentary film called *The Real Death Valley* about migrants who were dying in the harsh terrain of the South Texas brush country, I met Sigfredo Palomo, who had recently been released from a six-month stay at the Joe Corley ICE detention facility in Conroe, Texas, and was waiting for his asylum case to be heard. Sigfredo and his brother, Jose, had fled El Salvador's gang violence after their lives had been threatened.

Jose had been a prominent artist in San Salvador, and the notorious MS-13 gang had threatened him for not designing tattoos for its members. They had asked him repeatedly to draw designs for some of the gang leaders, and each time, he had refused. The gang had once beaten him nearly to death for this, and he had spent several weeks in the hospital. The gang had vowed that if he refused again, they would finish the job and kill him. Sigfredo had held a decent job as a car parts salesman for the Ford Motor Company in San Salvador. He had supported his wife and two kids—until the gangs began to extort him. With every sale that Sigfredo made, he had to pay the MS-13 gang a percentage of his commission. At first he had agreed just to keep the peace, but the rate kept increasing. When he couldn't make ends meet, his family suffered. He finally had enough and told his extortionists that he was done making payments. The following day, they followed him to work, and gang members showed up at his home, threating his wife and children.

After that, Sigfredo and Jose knew they couldn't stay in El Salvador a single day longer. Sigfredo moved his family in with his mother and hatched a plan with Jose, and the next morning, they headed away from all they had ever known toward the United States, a country they knew nothing about. Neither of them knew what they were going to do once they got where they were going; all they knew was that they had to leave.

Together, they made the difficult journey to the US-Mexico border, and with the aid of a coyote, they managed to cross into the country. But the most harrowing part came after they had crossed—when they came face-to-face with the cruelty and negligence of US policy and the extended arm of the US Border Patrol.[1]

- - -

US Border policy has always focused on more than just the boundaries between the United States and Mexico or Canada. The Immigration and Nationality Act of 1952 gave the US Border Patrol jurisdiction beyond the physical boundary lines of the country—it had authority up to a hundred miles into the interior. For decades, Border Patrol operated checkpoints up to this depth on major highways leading away from ports of entry as a secondary line of defense. It could stop motorists and ask for proof of legal residency. Since 9/11, amendments to the law have allowed more than just manning stationary checkpoints on highways. Border Patrol now has the authority to patrol neighborhoods within the hundred-mile-deep jurisdiction. It can use surveillance equipment, stop motorists, set up temporary checkpoints, make arrests, and monitor suspicious activity all within the hundred-mile zone from the US border.[2]

As its name suggests, Interior Customs Enforcement (popularly referred to as ICE) has similar police authority to the US Border Patrol, but it operates beyond the hundred-mile zone. ICE can enforce immigration law anywhere within the interior of the United States, including any part of Border Patrol's narrower jurisdiction. ICE and US Border Patrol collaborate on cases and law enforcement.[3] In addition to its policing power within the interior, ICE manages and operates a vast system of detention facilities for immigrants throughout the country.[4]

Border Patrol checkpoints are nothing new; as noted, they have existed for decades. What changed after 9/11 was the scrutiny of possible suspects crossing through them. The US government designated Border Patrol checkpoints as another place to look for would-be terrorists; at least, this is stated on the Border Patrol website: "The Border Patrol protects the United States by interdicting terrorists, illegal narcotics, and illegal aliens attempting to egress away from the border area into the interior portions of our nations [sic]."[5]

Surveillance was tightened, security infrastructure added, and technology revamped. What was once an opportunity for a border official to ask whether or not people driving through a checkpoint were US citizens became one for interrogating motorists and their passengers. Most individuals suspected of being terrorists have been brown, and they have received the heaviest scrutiny—at least according to those who oppose the very existence of the checkpoints.[6]

The US Border Patrol mans seventy-one checkpoints, including thirty-three permanent ones, up to seventy-five miles north of the US-Mexico border. The US Government Accountability

Office states that "the United States Supreme Court ruled that Border Patrol agents may stop a vehicle at fixed checkpoints for brief questioning of its occupants even if there is no reason to believe that the particular vehicle contains illegal aliens."[7]

The ACLU, as well as other civil rights groups, has argued that the Border Patrol checkpoints are unconstitutional and violate due process laws because agents are allowed to stop any vehicle or individual without probable cause. Everyone can be considered a possible undocumented immigrant or possible terrorist. Many opponents of the checkpoints, including the ACLU, believe that using a stop-all approach violates the Fourth Amendment, which protects Americans from random stops and searches.[8]

The arguments for the legality of the checkpoints may seem plausible, and such stops may appear necessary given the attacks of 9/11, but legal residents and US citizens who live near the border feel the effects of this attitude in their daily lives. Anyone living south of the checkpoint, if they have business north of it, is subject to inspection every single time they cross. For example, a father who is simply taking his child to school every morning or just picking up a carton of milk on the other side of the checkpoint is stopped and asked for legal residency status, and if an agent senses anything suspicious, the father, whether a US citizen or not, may be subject to an extensive search—every time, every day.

I have crossed through checkpoints hundreds of times, if not more. It feels like crossing through a militarized zone; it's not as innocuous as CBP describes it. There is usually a long line of cars waiting to interface with Border Patrol agents. As you approach, an array of cameras points at you and your vehicle. As you get closer, you might even see signs boasting about the number of "Pounds of Illegal Narcotics Seized" and "Illegal Aliens Apprehended"—a sort of scorecard of the checkpoint's efficacy.

You'll see a uniformed Border Patrol agent standing in the road and usually also drug-sniffing dogs that other agents walk around the vehicles approaching the checkpoint. If an agent sees something in your car that looks suspicious or suspects that you and/or your passengers are not legal residents, he or she can have you pull over to undergo a "secondary inspection" for a more thorough search and questioning. I have experienced this many times and have waited sometimes several hours for agents to inspect my vehicle. I have never heard a reason for it. At a checkpoint, I always look around to see which drivers have been stopped. The vast majority have brown faces.

According to the ACLU, "At checkpoints every day, border agents are unlawfully stopping, interrogating, and searching individuals with no suspicion of wrongdoing, and often in racially biased ways . . . . The government's dragnet approach to immigration and law enforcement both at the border and farther inland is one that turns us all into suspects."[9]

- - -

Since 9/11, the phenomenon of keeping migrants in detention as they learn their fates has exploded, and along with it the reliance on detention centers that private corporations such as CoreCivic and GEO Group run. About 70 percent of immigrants placed in detention are held for thirty days or less.[10] They are then usually deported—but immigration law is complicated, and the length of stay can depend on many factors. Immigrants who contest their arrest or claim asylum may languish for months or even years.[11]

It is difficult to determine which came first: the idea to incarcerate immigrants who claim asylum, argue their cases, or who are in the process of deportation—or private corporations lobbying the federal government nonstop to increase bed capacity and jail more immigrants. It is clear that detention periods have increased, bringing more profit for private holding facilities. In 2015, the average such stay for an immigrant was twenty-one days; in 2016, it was twenty-two; and in 2017, during the Trump administration, it shot up to thirty-four days, with over 70 percent of immigrants in privately run facilities—a ratio that continues to rise.[12]

In addition, it's hard to determine whether lobbyists from defense contractors to private prison corporations are responsible for America's zeal to secure the border or whether it is simply America wanting to wall herself off. In any case, it has created a feast for those who profit from the apprehension and incarceration of immigrants. Such profit models have expanded the war's front from the thin line at the US-Mexico border well into the interior of the United States. The country spends more to apprehend and incarcerate immigrants than any other in the world, and both government and profiteers have their hands in the till as budgets continue to climb and more and more immigrants are rounded up as a result.

In 1990, when border security really ramped up, the combined budget for the Border Patrol and customs agents was about $260 million.[13] Today, it hovers around $4 billion, a sixteenfold increase in about thirty years. If Trump gets his way, the current Customs and Border Protection budget will look like a bargain. Comparatively, the incarceration of immigrants has proven to stretch the budget of the federal government. In 1990, there were fewer than five thousand immigrants being detained at any given time, and today, over forty thousand sit in over two hundred facilities nationwide. Texas, California, and Arizona, because they are along the Mexico border, have most of the detention facilities, but every state in the nation has at least two.[14]

In 2010, when Congress allocated funding for privatizing immigrant detention, the cost to the program was $1.7 billion. Today, it has nearly doubled to over $3 billion. The costs and the number of private corporations lining up at the immigrant dollar trough continue to grow. Did the border security industry grow because more immigrants were crossing the border, or merely as an opportunity for profiteers to line their pockets?

It's worth noting that the growth of detention centers continued unabated during President Barack Obama's first term
and much of his second. At a gala in 2014, Janet Murguía, president of the National Council of La Raza (NCLR), a powerful
Latino lobbying organization, said of Obama, "For us, this president has been the deporter-in-chief."[15] Obama continued the
legacy of all US presidents and administrations since Ronald
Reagan, making life more difficult for immigrants. Obama's rate
of deportation of immigrants already established in the country
was higher than that of any president before or since. During
his eight years in office, Obama deported more than five million
people, and so far, even Trump has not beat that record.[16]

Obama also expanded family detention facilities for women
with their children. As a response to an influx of thousands of
Central Americans fleeing violence and poverty, some seeking
asylum at the border, the Obama administration built new family detention facilities in Texas as a deterrent to keep more from
coming. The image of jailed women and children was supposed
to send the message of an unwelcoming nation. Many believe
that the detention of children, albeit with their mothers, is the
most egregious immigration-related stain on the Obama record.

It is well documented that politicians who support high
border security are supported handsomely, with generous campaign contributions from defense contractors. The aerospace
and defense giant Lockheed Martin donated $127,000 to Pres-
ident Barack Obama's reelection campaign in 2012.[17] It also
gave $49,500 to Senator Charles Schumer (D-NY), the con-
gressman spearheading the comprehensive immigration reform
effort with the "gang of eight" in the Senate in 2012.[18] Boeing,
another company that received a billion-dollar border security
infrastructure contract, donated in 2012 to Senator Lindsey
Graham (R-SC) amounting to $16,500[19] and gave $10,000 to
Robert Menendez (D-NJ).[20] Boeing gave roughly $191,000 to
President Obama.[21] Both Lockheed Martin and Boeing are at
the top of political giving, and both have received vast amounts

in federal contracts. During the 2013 debate over comprehensive immigration reform, lobbyists helped add $40 billion[22] in border security amendments to the bill—which never passed.[23]

For years, Congress has appropriated more dollars for border security infrastructure without many safeguards to prove that the extra money is actually securing the border. There are no metrics to determine whether or not the dollars have kept the country safe or kept immigrants from entering illegally. In 2018, Lockheed Martin received over $22 billion in federal contracts—the highest amount of any company.[24] Unsurprisingly, it also has a stake in border security, with a $106 million contract for aircraft and data processing.[25]

This pattern of increased militarization in one form or another seems to have repeated with every new administration since Reagan—with more and more infrastructure, more guards, and more detention facilities. The border has been fortified and militarized, making it harder for migrants to cross but never stopping them from trying. Very few politicians take stands to challenge the militarization of the border. In addition to more border security infrastructure, since 9/11, detention centers and the industry associated with them have grown at an increasing rate through the 2010s.

- - -

Once Sigfredo and Jose had decided to leave for the United States, they needed $5,000 each to hire a coyote to get them safely across the border. They cobbled together money by draining their bank accounts and borrowing the rest. The brothers handled their own journey through Mexico, but they didn't want to get stuck at the border. The goal was Houston.

Sigfredo and Jose took a series of trains and buses to Reynosa, Mexico, a border town near McAllen, Texas, where security was especially tight. The buildup since 9/11 had been massive; the US government had spent millions in this region to keep the likes of Sigfredo and Jose out. By the time the brothers arrived, there were already twenty miles of wall blocking access to the city of McAllen. Since then, the Trump administration has suggested another forty-five miles of barrier. There is also a proposed LED lighting system and a camera array for atop the walls capable of monitoring a 150-foot radius day and night. In fiscal year 2017, Congress appropriated $1.6 billion for border security infrastructure, including at McAllen.[26] But it is likely that the cartels will find a way around the additional buildup just as they did when Sigfredo and Jose crossed.

The brothers were determined to get in or die trying. This was their last resort. No matter the obstacle, no matter the price, they were going to make it. Dollars and militarization were no match for two desperate men fleeing violence and certain death and seeking an opportunity to support their families from the United States.

Guided by the coyote, who was with the Zeta cartel, Sigfredo and Jose managed to cross into the United States by swimming the Rio Grande River undetected. Wet and tired, the two men stayed in a safe house on the outskirts of McAllen until other migrants showed up. It had become a common practice to wait in a hidden location after crossing the border; "move and hide" was a proven tactic to keep border officials off immigrants' trail. Sigfredo and Jose slept on that concrete floor for a few days. Jose woke up one morning achy, and his head hurt a bit—a flu, probably. The brothers were emotionally exhausted and tired from the journey, but a little flu wouldn't dampen their spirits. In a day or two, they would leave McAllen and head into the interior of the country.

There was one more obstacle the brothers had to overcome, and after all they had been through, it seemed insignificant. Between McAllen and the freedom of Houston was a Border Patrol checkpoint about seventy miles to the north in a small ranch town called Falfurrias. As in other regions along the border, it served as a secondary line of defense. All vehicles must stop, and agents ask passengers for their immigration status before they move any farther. Smugglers know this is a risky place to drive through with a carload of migrants since Border Patrol targets mostly brown people for inspection. To avoid detection, smugglers often drop migrants off at a point about ten miles south. The migrants then walk about thirty miles north of the checkpoint—a total of forty miles on foot. They finally rendezvous with a pickup car. The forty-mile journey took three or more days. This would be Sigfredo and Jose's route as well.

The brothers thought this was going to be easy. A few days of walking—and then freedom from all the horrors they had known. No matter how hot or how hard the conditions, their resolve would get them through. About five hundred migrants made this trek every day. How hard could it be?

After a few days at the safe house, the coyote and a group of six migrants, including Sigfredo and Jose, packed into a car and went from McAllen to south of the Falfurrias checkpoint in South Texas. Under the cover of darkness, the group was dumped onto a farm road and told to follow a series of power lines that stretched for miles. They would head out into open terrain, walking day and night up to Highway 141.

Their very first task was to scale a fifteen-foot wire fence meant to keep game animals in and migrants out. Sigfredo, Jose, and the others would have to scale many of these game fences as they made their way north. This area was a popular destination for hunting vacations—as well as for undocumented immigrants trying to evade the checkpoint. It was the same general area where former Vice President Dick Cheney had shot his buddy in the face while they hunted quail.

For the first night, all were in good spirits. They had made it into the United States and were now on the last leg of their journey. In a few days, they would all be safely on the other side of the last security checkpoint and in a car headed to Houston. Past the checkpoint, the odds of border officials detecting them greatly diminished. Agents could only patrol about a hundred miles north of the border, and Houston was well beyond their reach. The new arrivals might have to contend with ICE agents once they reached Houston, but that was not their primary concern.

Sigfredo and Jose walked briskly with the group. They made good time, although after about ten miles, the midday sun would beat down on them and slow their progress. The two brothers dreamed aloud of their new life in the United States—of the jobs they would find, the money they could send back home, and maybe even being able to send for their families later. They sang American tunes and discussed having cheeseburgers once they got to Houston.

As the sun rose the following morning, Jose was slower, wheezing a bit. The congestion and runny nose he had experienced in the safe house were now getting worse. He had a headache and felt like he was running a low fever. His body hurt, but he wasn't sure if it was from sleeping on the concrete floor, walking all night, or just being ill. He asked the guide if he could sit for a few minutes and drink some water. The guide allowed the group a break, but he told Jose, "Drink fast and don't get too comfortable. The longer we're here, the easier it is to get caught."

Jose took long gulps of water from his gallon jug and sat for only a couple of minutes, catching his breath. Sigfredo noticed that his brother was sweating more profusely than everyone else, but he wasn't too concerned. Jose was young and healthy, only twenty-one years old. He would have no problem continuing, even if he had the flu. The coyote rallied everyone to start the trek again. Jose stood, almost losing his balance. He told Sigfredo that he might need a little help and leaned on him as they started walking again.

The day was hot and getting hotter. The trek had seemed as if it would be easy, since the land was flat and in places, there were tall trees for shade. But walking on the sandy soil, once an ancient sea floor, was grueling. The heavy, thick sand made every step a struggle. It was more taxing on the body than hiking on rocks or even climbing. Jose did not last long before he asked the guide if he could rest again. The guide said no, they had to keep moving. Sigfredo told him to shake it off and quit thinking about how bad he felt—to think instead about the freedom of Houston. Sigfredo said, "Just a few more hours, and we'll be there. Just push through, you can make it." The truth was, the group still had probably two more days to go.

Jose sat himself down on the sandy ground under a tree; despite the guide's warnings and Sigfredo's stern pep talk, he needed to rest. He was drenched in sweat and breathing heavily. The coyote quickly noticed and headed for him. "If you don't get up right now, you're staying behind."

Sigfredo tried to lift Jose up, but he sat limp. "I need a few minutes," Jose said. The guide didn't even look back. He told the remaining three migrants to follow him, and they quickly disappeared into the thick brush.

"We're going to be left behind. Come on, let's go!" Sigfredo was able to rally Jose, who slowly got up on his feet and began to follow the guide, who by now was several yards ahead.

– – –

Brooks County, Texas, where the brothers were crossing, was no stranger to migrant traffic. The tactic of walking through ranch land to evade the checkpoint had become frequent there. Even migrant deaths were common. The year before Sigfredo and Jose crossed the border, 121 bodies had been recovered in this small county—that is, the ones that were found.[27] Experts estimated that there could have been ten times that amount. No one was really out there looking for migrant remains. Even if a Border Patrol agent noticed bones, I heard that they wouldn't bother examining them. Bones scattered the landscape, since there were so many cattle on it and game hunters often left their prey to rot. Border Patrol would have to come upon an intact skeleton or a human skull to count it as a real migrant death. Migrant bodies turn to bone quickly in this climate, being eaten by carnivores and insects alike. Predators scatter the bones of the dead, so finding human remains or even a skeleton intact is unlikely just a few weeks after death. Bones of human beings are likely to litter the ranches of South Texas for years to come, never to be identified properly.

The county sheriff's department at that time consisted of one sheriff and four deputies. It did not have the personnel to handle migrant traffic or deaths. The Border Patrol agents who managed the checkpoint were responsible for migrants crossing the ranch land, and the sheriff's department solicited their aid in search and rescue if it heard of a migrant in distress. The Border Patrol had beefed up its security in this area as it had at every other checkpoint and port of entry along the border. Several hundred agents combed the ranch lands for migrants, and they would answer the 911 calls from migrants who happened to have cell phones once the sheriff relayed them. The Border Patrol station helped pinpoint calls with GPS.

The Border Patrol had all the vehicles, dogs, helicopters, and trained personnel to do rescues. Border Search Trauma and Rescue (BORSTAR), specially trained Border Patrol agents for search and rescue, were among the personnel stationed in Brooks County.

After several years of experience in the field, Border Patrol agents can apply to become search and rescue personnel—these are considered elite members of the patrol. Medical training and long classroom hours prepare these specialized agents for the field. In addition, "BORSTAR agents receive advanced specialized training in emergency medical; tactical medicine; paramedic; austere medic; helicopter rope suspension training; rescue watercraft/boat operator; cold-weather training and more." [28] So the US government created a system of deterrence that has forced migrants into dangerous territory, and then it created an elite force to rescue migrants in distress.

The then sheriff of Brooks County, Chief Benny Martinez, was the one who told me that he just did not have the personnel or equipment to handle all the migrants in distress walking around the checkpoint in his county. He didn't like it, but he had to rely on the Border Patrol to address the issue. "Too many people die in this county, and I need the help." But he didn't think that the Border Patrol always did its job well. He agreed that the agents were busy apprehending evasive migrants, but they seemed to take their time to look for any who were distressed and even near death. He was never sure when they would actually respond to his relayed 911 calls, if ever. He said that migrants in distress did not seem to be a priority, even though the Border Patrol had agreed to be an emergency first responder in Brooks County. Fellow residents of Brooks County echoed his sentiment when I spoke with many of them. They said that agents would leave ailing migrants in the brush to die, because they didn't want the hassle of rescuing people or of hospital paperwork. Most residents I spoke to said that Border Patrol simply had a disdain for migrants and that rescuing them was of little interest.

It was almost night, yet there didn't seem to be much relief from the heat. The day had become progressively hotter and more humid. Jose tried to keep up with the group, and Sigfredo kept encouraging him to keep moving, saying that it was only just a little bit farther. By now, though, they had lost sight of the group. Sigfredo knew that if they followed certain power lines, they would eventually make it to the road where they were supposed to be picked up and driven to Houston. He also knew that if they didn't keep moving, they might not make their pickup time and could be left behind, to be stranded for who knows how long.

As darkness fell, Jose took a turn for the worse. He just sat down on a rock and didn't speak. He didn't move or talk, just sat there. Sigfredo tried one more time to encourage him, but he noticed Jose's blank stare. This was bad. Sigfredo, without thinking, called 911, connecting with the Brooks County Sheriff's department. He told the dispatcher that he was lost in the brush and that his brother, Jose, was very ill and needed help immediately. The dispatcher quickly jotted down the information and relayed it to the Border Patrol station, which told the Brooks County dispatcher that agents would be out within forty-five minutes. The dispatcher called Sigfredo back and told him to stay put and that help was on the way.

Sigfredo was relieved, as Jose's condition was deteriorating by the minute. He knew that calling 911 would most likely get the two arrested and deported, but he couldn't let his brother die. This was a call he had had to make. He did as instructed and waited, but no one arrived. After ninety minutes, still no one showed up. Even though the men had stopped walking, Jose was not getting any better. Sigfredo decided to call 911 again and say that no one had arrived. The dispatcher called the Border Patrol again and heard that they had gotten the wrong coordinates but would arrive within an hour. Sigfredo was relieved, sure that help would arrive.

That next hour passed slowly, and Jose began to get delirious. He had bouts of shouting and crying, and then he would rest and fall into what appeared to be a deep sleep. Two hours went by, and no Border Patrol vehicles arrived. Sigfredo called 911 again and told the dispatcher that his brother was getting sicker and sicker and that they needed to hurry. The dispatcher was surprised that the Border Patrol had not yet arrived and called it again.

Over the course of several hours, Jose's condition worsened. Sigfredo made five 911 calls over the span of eight hours, and the Border Patrol never arrived.

Jose began to scream incoherently at Sigfredo. He was like
a crazed man, making sudden movements left and right and
throwing himself to the ground with force. Sigfredo tried to
hold him and console him, but Jose didn't even recognize him
and would break free only to continue the erratic behavior. In
one last burst of energy, Jose shouted, convulsed, and fell to the
ground. He was dead.

Sigfredo refused to believe it. He kept trying to revive his
brother, telling him that he couldn't die, that they need to take
care of their family, that they were going to make it together. He
held Jose, weeping.

Within minutes, Sigfredo was back on his feet. He didn't
know what to do except call 911 again—his sixth call. Barely
able to speak and full of emotion, he told the dispatcher that
his brother had just died and that no one had come. The dispatcher was stunned that the Border Patrol had never showed
up. The sheriff handles deceased individuals, so the dispatcher
relayed the information to the deputy on call that evening. It
was the county sheriff who quickly found Sigfredo and Jose,
using the exact coordinates that the Border Patrol had received
many hours earlier.

As protocol dictates, whenever the Brooks County sheriff
finds an undocumented immigrant in the field, it notifies the US
Border Patrol—which the deputy did when he found Sigfredo
and Jose. The Border Patrol finally arrived to arrest Sigfredo
while the deputy handled the recovery of Jose's remains. The
Border Patrol agent who apprehended Sigfredo did not offer
any explanation of why no one had responded to the repeated
911 calls, nor did he offer condolences for the dead brother.
He said only that Sigfredo would be placed in temporary custody, moved to a detention facility, and deported. At this point,
Sigfredo didn't care where he was going or what was going to
happen to him. He was in shock.

Unfortunately, this case was no anomaly. A year's worth of
911 calls to the Brooks County Sheriff's Department revealed

that the average response time for US Border Patrol to a migrant in distress was over two and a half hours. In some cases, as with Sigfredo and Jose, the wait times were as high as eight or nine hours, and in some as high as fourteen. The average response time for a US citizen in similar rural areas is less than twenty minutes.[29] Sheriff Benny Martinez thought that the Border Patrol should be able to find migrants with good coordinates in about thirty minutes. The US Border Patrol did not take its role in Brooks County as an emergency first responder very seriously. Migrants in distress did not appear to be enough of a priority to expedite rescue efforts. Sheriff Martinez's hands were tied. He didn't have the resources or manpower to handle the nearly nightly distress calls. He had to rely on the almost two hundred Border Patrol agents in his area—and they were negligent in saving the lives of migrants.

- - -

Within days of fleeing from El Salvador and losing his brother, Sigfredo found himself in the Joe Corley Detention Center outside Houston, Texas—an ironic contrast to his hope of a final destination. This detention facility operates under the guidelines of ICE, which, again, now has more than twenty thousand employees in over four hundred offices throughout the country and an annual budget of $4 billion. ICE also manages detention facilities directly.[30]

Nearly every year since 2001 has broken new records in the number of detainees. When Sigfredo arrived there in 2014, there were over thirty thousand individuals in detention annually. The number has only risen since: in 2018, ICE detention facilities held more than 42,000 individuals on any given day and over 360,000 immigrants annually.[31] In early 2019, Congress allocated more funding to increase capacity.

Of the hundreds of detention facilities that ICE manages, 71 percent belong to private, for-profit prison corporations like

Geo Group, which owns Sigfredo's former facility, and Core-
Civic Inc. (previously known as Corrections Corporation of
America).[32] These two companies hold more than half of all US
detention facility contracts. Ten years ago, most bed space had
been obtained at jails and state prisons. That's where Sigfredo
would have been then, and if he had had no immigration claims
or criminal violations, he would have been sent back to El Salvador within a few weeks. Now most migrants with removal
orders wait at least a month before deportation, which allows
the privately owned facilities to run up their tabs on the federal
government. Combined earned income for private detention
facilities in 2017 reached $4 billion. This is a booming industry
that seeks more facilities as it rounds up more immigrants for
"mandatory detention" each year, especially since Trump took
office. In 2016, ICE apprehended 415,816 people, an increase of
23 percent over fiscal year 2015. ICE reported a 17 percent drop
in apprehensions in 2017 and touts its own effectiveness as a
reason.[33]

Analysts have well documented that privately run detention
facilities are more expensive to operate than government-run
facilities and that cutting corners to maximize profits has
resulted in shoddy conditions and care.[34] When I met Sigfredo,
he had already been in the private detention facility for months.
While there, he had decided to claim asylum, which he hadn't
known was an option at the time of his arrest. Then he edu-
cated himself on US asylum law and found that those fleeing
gang violence in Central America could qualify. But the process
is long and tedious. Asylum seekers must gather evidence of
persecution based on their religious beliefs, political leanings,
or sexual orientation and prove that they feared for their lives.
Wait times for immigration judges to hear cases can be more
than a year, often still in a detention facility. Sigfredo's proof that
he had faced imminent death could be in the form of testimony
from his family, friends, and coworkers as well as any verifiable
evidence that he had been a target of the gangs in El Salvador.

While he was in custody, he was able to contact his family and some business associates to get the process rolling, though his calls back home were limited to one a day. He also let his family know that Jose had passed. Gathering evidence for his case was difficult, coupled with the fact that he felt responsible for his brother's death and was left to grieve alone. At least the process of putting his paperwork together and waiting for his day in court kept him busy while incarcerated.

Asylum seekers can qualify for release until their court date if they can post bail—which can run as high as $10,000–$20,000 or more, depending on the judge or the circumstances of the asylum seeker—and prove that they can be remanded to a sponsor or family member who can vouch for their whereabouts. Sigfredo had a sister in the United States, but neither of them could post the bail of $12,500.

Sigfredo told me about how the employees of the detention facility treated him like a criminal. He said they regularly degraded and insulted him. I had investigated similar accounts of negligence, malfeasance, and corner cutting in such facilities. Many migrants complained of substandard medical care, poor food quality, and racially insensitive treatment by trained staff. Attorneys and legal organizations like the ACLU and Human Rights Watch have documented and filed suits against detention facilities for the abuse, mistreatment, and even suspicious deaths of migrant inmates, yet every authorized ICE facility has passed every inspection since 2012—even those where multiple people have died (some later reported as resulting from medical neglect), and none have ever lost their license to operate.[35]

Gerardo Cruz-Sanchez was trying to cross the border near Nogales, Arizona, when Border Patrol agents caught him in the desert. He remained in their custody for a few days and caught a cold; he was then transferred to the Otay Mesa ICE detention facility belonging to CoreCivic Inc., outside of San Diego, California. According to court documents, Cruz had been a healthy man when he entered the detention facility in early

2016; two weeks later, he was dead. He had contracted pneumonia while in custody. Several days after he had been admitted, Cruz began to feel ill. He was vomiting and had terrible chills and night sweats. He must have known he was getting worse. He requested medical care, which is every detainee's right, but his cellmate, Alejandro Chavez, stated that Cruz received only aspirin and was never allowed to see a doctor.

Records show that cellmate Chavez made over thirty calls to the Mexican consulate to sound the alarm that Cruz was dying.[36] Chavez also pleaded for help with the detention facility staff but said that they told him that Cruz "needed to be near death" before he would be hospitalized. Cruz was near unconsciousness and covered in sweat when he was finally sent to a hospital, where he died two days later from complications of pneumonia. While he was in ICE custody, no doctor ever examined him.[37]

"More people died in immigration detention in fiscal year 2017 than any year since 2009, and the most recent detailed information we have about immigration detention deaths shows that they are still linked to dangerously inadequate medical care,"[38] states a Human Rights Watch report issued in 2018. Poor medical treatment contributed to more than half the deaths that ICE reported during a sixteen-month period.

Human Rights Watch obtained medical records that independent physicians then examined. There was evidence of substandard medical practices in all but one of the remaining reviews. "ICE has proven unable or unwilling to provide adequately for the health and safety of the people it detains," said Clara Long, a senior US researcher at Human Rights Watch. "The Trump administration's efforts to drastically expand the already-bloated immigration detention system will only put more people at risk." Since March 2010, eighty-two people have died in immigration detention. Since 2003, more than 188 people have died in immigrant detention. We have seen that there have been substantial casualties of the war on the border, and now in the interior and in immigrant jails.[39] Again, my reporting has shown that no ICE facility that detains immigrants has shut down or had its license withdrawn.

The rapid expansion of detention facilities, combined with increasing budgets, has created a sprawling system that seems to have little oversight or true accountability. As a result, the number of detainees has grown dramatically. The average daily population of detained immigrants increased from approximately five thousand in 1994 to nineteen thousand in 2001, and to over forty thousand in 2018. The Trump administration has asked for funding to detain as many as fifty-two thousand.[40]

- - -

After six months in detention, Sigfredo received some good news. He had found an organization willing to help him post the $12,500 he needed for bail. He would be able to live with his sister while he waited for his asylum case to be adjudicated. He was not allowed to travel, nor did he have an opportunity to work right away. Every day, he worried about his family back in El Salvador. Sigfredo had attracted a pro-bono legal group to take his case. His lawyer told me that even with legal representation, Sigfredo had a less than a one-in-ten chance of gaining asylum, but without it, his odds would have been worse. Unfortunately, the courts do not provide legal assistance to immigrants in detention facilities; they must obtain it on their own. Most, however, do not find affordable attorneys and end up being deported simply because they don't understand their rights or the maze of immigration laws.

A year later, Sigfredo is still waiting for a decision about his case and hasn't seen his wife or kids in all that time. He still carries the cross that Jose was wearing when they crossed the border, touching it constantly to remind himself that Jose is watching over him.

8

Trump

When Donald Trump took office on January 20, 2017, he gained control of a massively militarized border and a Department of Homeland Security that had unprecedented power. By then, the department had a budget of over $70 billion; Border Patrol officers numbered around twenty thousand. As noted, ICE had about that many employees in four hundred offices throughout the country and over two hundred immigrant detention facilities—there were at least two in every state. Seventy-one border patrol checkpoints dotted the region along the southern border. There were seven hundred miles of fencing along the border with Mexico—none along the Canadian border. On average, nearly fifty thousand immigrants were in detention centers—the most in the world. About 750,000 immigration cases waited to be adjudicated, with an average wait time for a hearing of over two years.[1]

For many concerned about the state of US immigration, the election of Donald J. Trump spelled catastrophe. He opened his campaign by labeling Mexicans as "rapists" and called for building a border wall that Mexico would pay for. He vowed to protect America by deporting those who were criminal, saying at a rally in Miami, "A Trump administration will stop illegal immigration, deport all criminal aliens, and save American lives."[2] His demonization of immigrants struck a chord with millions of Americans. Of course, his anti-immigrant rhetoric was not entirely new. Bill Clinton's 1995 State of the Union address was one Trump could have delivered: "That's why our administration has moved aggressively to secure our borders more by hiring a record number of new border guards, by deporting twice as many criminal aliens as ever before." Presidents and members of Congress before him had contributed to an atmosphere where threatening to come down hard against immigrants was politically expedient. For decades, immigrants had been portrayed as threats to our national security and to US workers.

Nor was Trump the first to call for a wall—or even to begin building one. As I've noted, the first real border walls between the United States and Mexico went up in the early 1990s. San Diego and El Paso were the first to see the metal panels constructed, and other parts of Texas and Arizona were next. After 9/11, an additional seven hundred miles of border barriers rose during the Bush administration, and the Obama administration maintained them through congressional votes and budget agreements. The only thing that Trump did differently was to be bold and brash about it. He made no apologies for wanting to build a continuous wall. His rhetoric was not nuanced; neither did he mince words about who he thought America's enemies were—south of the border and abroad.

Trump's predecessors had laid the groundwork and built up the infrastructure. Once in the White House, Trump put his anti-immigrant campaign rhetoric into practice. Congress gave Trump no new immigration laws, though; the president used solely what was already at his disposal in previous legislation. In his first two years, he has escalated the war against immigrants and the militarization of the border to a level above that of any president before him.

Among his many campaign promises and pronouncements against immigrants, he planned to issue a ban against Muslims until he figured out "what the hell is going on." Once installed as president, on January 24, 2017, Trump issued restrictions on travel from seven different countries with large Muslim populations: Iran, Libya, North Korea, Somalia, Venezuela, and Yemen.[3] There was an immediate backlash from immigrant communities and nations worldwide. The ban also created immediate panic at airports, with people being stranded and not allowed to travel even on legal visas they already had. The implementation of the ban was sloppy and intentionally punitive. Within a few weeks, the state of Washington filed a suit against the federal government, saying, "The order destabilizes and fundamentally alters the lives of many Washington residents and their families."[4] The Ninth Circuit Court of Appeals agreed and halted portions of the ban, citing that the restrictions had been placed on predominantly Muslim countries, an unconstitutional action.[5] The Trump administration fought back by editing the list of countries and types of restrictions for each to make the order more palatable for the courts, and in June 2018, the Supreme Court ruled in favor of the Trump administration with restrictions for Muslim countries altogether remaining.[6]

In 2018, the Trump administration cut the staff that conducts clearance interviews overseas and intensified the screening process for refugees from the banned countries. As a result, only twenty thousand refugees were expected by the end of that year[7]—the lowest figure since the resettlement program created with the Refugee Act in 1980. The restrictions have also caused a steep decline in Muslim immigrants to the United States. In fiscal year 2016, 38,900 Muslim refugees came to the country, according to the State Department. In 2017, the number fell to 22,861. Only 2,107 entered in the first six months of 2018.

On April 18, 2017, Trump signed an executive order asking the Department of Homeland Security to review the H-1B program to make sure that only highly skilled immigrants received these foreign-worker visas. What followed was a 45 percent surge in applicants, a 15 percent increase in fees, and faster denials.[8] Only time will tell if higher scrutiny of foreign workers and more costly visas translates into a better workforce. Trump's rhetoric was that he wanted to deny visas to anyone who might undercut the salaries of US-born residents.[9] The order was seemingly directed at Indian firms like Tata Consultancy, Infosys, and Wipro, which are located in the United States but hire many immigrants from India. But the temporary visa program helps employ up to 315,000 in the computer and tech industries with some of America's most profitable companies in Silicon Valley, who are concerned that visa restrictions will hurt their bottom lines.[10] Facebook and Qualcomm are big users of the program; 15 percent of their workers are H-1B immigrants.

In Trump's address to a joint session of Congress in 2017, he announced the establishment of the Victims of Immigration Crime Engagement to assist the victims of crimes specifically committed by removable criminal aliens. "I have ordered the Department of Homeland Security to create an office to serve American victims," Trump said. "We are providing a voice to those who have been ignored by our media, and silenced by special interests."[11] The "Objectives" of the initiative stated on the Department of Homeland Security website seem to conflate immigrants and criminals:

Objectives

1. Use a victim-centered approach to acknowledge and support immigration crime victims and their families.
2. Promote awareness of rights and services available to immigration crime victims.
3. Build collaborative partnerships with community stakeholders assisting immigration crime victims.
4. Provide quarterly reports studying the effects of the victimization by criminal aliens present in the United States.

The understanding that the executive order seems to promote is that crimes that immigrants commit are especially heinous because they could easily have been prevented if the perpetrators had been deported earlier or never allowed in the country to begin with.

On June 22, 2017, Trump asked Congress to prevent all immigrants from receiving welfare for their first five years in the country. Although the Clinton administration had placed similar restrictions on immigrants in 1996, Trump vowed to scrap any exemptions left in that bill. The move would take authority away from states, which currently decide who is eligible for assistance programs. The administration would also be allowed to enforce regulations that deny immigration status to those who seem likely to become "public charges" within the first five years of their arrival, reinforcing the notion that immigrants are a drain on society.

On August 2, 2017, the Trump administration endorsed a Senate bill that curbs legal immigration. It prioritizes those who are financially self-sufficient, highly skilled, and speak English. It denies green cards to adult children and extended relatives of current green card holders. If the bill became law, it would reduce the number of green cards issued from one million to 638,000 in its first year.[12] So far, the bill has not even made it to the floor for a vote. In September 2018, the administration also pushed to restrict green cards from immigrants who have sought public assistance such as food stamps and Section 8 housing vouchers—targeting poor and elderly immigrants. If this were to be enforced, nearly four hundred thousand green card holders would be affected.[13]

Trump has also canceled the Deferred Action for Childhood Arrivals (DACA) program, which is currently providing work authorization and temporary relief from deportation to approximately 690,000 unauthorized immigrants brought to the United States as children. Although the battle to keep Dreamers legal and in the United States is currently running through the courts, the protections for minors who came to the country illegally through no fault of their own are tenuous at best. The administration has also ended the designation of "temporary protected status" for nationals of Haiti, Nicaragua, Sudan, and Vietnam and signaled that Hondurans and possibly Salvadorans may also lose their work authorization and protection from removal in 2019, although the measure remains tied up in the courts.[14] This would suggest that nearly 350,000 immigrants from Central America could lose their right to live and work in the United States.[15] Many of them have lived in the country for years and have built lives that would be uprooted—and on top of that, these people gained their temporary protected status because of hardships they suffered in their home countries. The revocation would send them back, in many cases, to countries that are now worse off than when they left.

In the two years since Trump has been in office, his administration has also reversed the decline in arrests of unauthorized immigrants in the US interior that occurred during the last two years of the Obama administration. In April 2018, the Trump administration announced a zero-tolerance policy at the US-Mexico border and in the US interior.[16] Simply put, all immigration laws that could be enforced would be, regardless of circumstances. About a year prior to that announcement, the Trump administration suggested they would be "taking the shackles off" law enforcement.[17] If caught in the interior, immigrants who had once been considered as posing no threat would be deported regardless of whether they had committed crimes or had established families and jobs.

ICE officials began to stake out hospitals, schools, and courthouses, places where undocumented immigrants felt safe to conduct their lives. ICE "policy [was] meant to ensure that ICE officers and agents exercise sound judgment when enforcing federal law at or focused on sensitive locations and make substantial efforts to avoid unnecessarily alarming local communities,"[18] suggesting that it would not apprehend migrants in these locations for public safety reasons. Theoretically, undocumented immigrants could access these necessary services important to daily life, but instead, lawyers on the ground, arrest records, and video evidence indicated that ICE was violating its own protocols. There is video of a young girl filming her father being deported as she sat in a car waiting to be dropped off at school.[19] In it, she is heard crying as her father is handcuffed and placed in an unmarked ICE vehicle.

Similar video emerged of a raid on a mechanic's shop in Los Angeles, where ICE agents posed as local police.[20] They entered the business with automatic weapons drawn, even though there had been no report of anyone armed or dangerous inside. Six people were arrested; three of them were US citizens. Alejandro Hernandez, an undocumented immigrant who had been living in the United States for twenty years with his wife and their daughter, a US citizen, was among them. Hernandez later told me that he had no idea what was going on. No one ever showed him a badge or an arrest warrant. Records indicate that ICE officials had obtained no warrant to search the premises; nor did LAPD approve their posing as police officers. Hernandez told me that he was handcuffed and placed in an unmarked car without ever hearing why he was being arrested. He had no idea that these were ICE agents and that they were arresting him for immigration violations. Once at the ICE processing facility, he realized why he was in custody. The procedures that the agents used in the arrest were in violation of protocol and Fourth Amendment protections. The ACLU quickly took on the case; Hernandez was released within days and allowed to remain in the country. The federal government did not contest accusations of its violation of due process or proper procedure.

One of the most potent effects of the Trump administration's zero tolerance to date has been its family separation policy. As a reaction to 9/11, the Bush administration, made it okay to prosecute border crossers. What used to be an administrative offense to cross the border without papers, punishable mostly by deportation, now had the possibility of becoming a felony in criminal court.[21] Such a conviction would bar an immigrant from eligibility to apply for legal status in the future. It must be

noted that although the Bush administration gave itself the freedom to prosecute anyone crossing the border without papers, it
didn't enforce the law to its full extent. But the fact that crossing the border could become a felony gave the Trump administration an open door to separate children from their parents.
Still, the Bush administration made that possible, not Trump.

In 2018, the Trump administration sought to put the punitive
immigration laws to full effect. In March of that year, reports
from the border suggested that children were being removed
from parents who were apprehended at the border either seeking asylum or illegal access to the United States. The federal
government was relying on the aforementioned felony laws,
which allow law enforcement to separate children from their
parents if they are in the commission of a crime. Since crossing
the border was a potential felony, the removal of children was
deemed legal, and the Trump administration took full advantage. The fact that asylum seekers were also being charged was
highly irregular and possibly illegal, but that became a matter
for the courts. Any migrant with children in tow was in danger
of being separated from them, based on settled law. On paper,
the Trump administration had the alleged legal right to demand
such a draconian policy be implemented across the board. It
admitted that the enforcement strategy was meant to send a
threatening message to those coming to the US border.

The separation of children from their parents caused an
outcry. Thousands of kids were moved to makeshift shelters
across the country, and matching kids with their parents after
they faced deportation became a boondoggle. The administration failed to reunite nearly six hundred children. They lost
track of their parents after many had been deported. Most of
those kids remained in the United States, and eventually, the
Department of Health and Human Services or foster care took
charge of them.

By order of the executive branch, Customs and Border Protection implemented these policies often just to look tough on

border issues. The Bush administration had introduced Operation Streamline post 9/11 to penalize migrants en masse. The apprehended were all shackled together and lined up before a judge to enter a plea. If they pled guilty, they would be deported; if not, they would remain in detention, sometimes indefinitely. Most migrants pled guilty and had felonies placed on their records, barring them for life from legal residency in the United States.

When these Bush administration sentencing guidelines allowed the Trump administration to levy felonies on every border crosser, children being removed from parents was only a side effect. No law had been written to allow this action specifically. In the past, first-time border crossers were simply deported, and repeat offenders could receive a penalty. The Trump administration saw that it could charge even first-time offenders with a felony, so it did. The rhetoric was that once the parents had their day in court, if they qualified, they could reunite with their children upon release. As long as parents remained in custody, they could not reunite with their kids, who, again, had been scattered across the country in shelters. The courts actually cited the administration for this, mandating it to return all children to their parents. But, as I've noted, it couldn't.[22]

The Trump administration clearly knew that it did not have to separate children from their parents just because it had a legal right to do so. The Obama administration had established family detention facilities to keep families together while they waited for outcomes in their immigration cases. Trump administration memos suggest that it had discussed the possibility of separating children from parents for about a year before then chief of staff John Kelly implemented the policy.[23] They knew what they were doing, and they did it on purpose.

The idea of separating children from their families conjures up images of horror, but what received less reporting was that profitmongers showed up to make money off the tragic policy blunder. Just like defense contractors showing up at the border to make their billions "keeping America safe," other contractors benefited from housing children and their parents. In a *New York Times* in-depth investigative report, Manny Fernandez and Katie Benner detail the profits expertly, declaring that housing migrant children quickly became a billion-dollar business.[24] Warehouses and even former Walmart stores were quickly converted into shelters.

Several large defense contractors and security firms vied for the billion-dollar contract including General Dynamics, the global aerospace and defense company, and MVM Inc., which until 2008 had contracted with the government to supply guards in Iraq. MVM put up postings seeking "bilingual travel youth care workers" in the McAllen area of South Texas, describing its jobs as providing care to immigrant children "while you are accompanying them on domestic flights and via ground transportation to shelters all over the country."[25]

The Obama administration had received strong criticism for housing women and children in what were deemed family detention facilities after they were hit with a massive wave of Central Americans fleeing increasing violence from the region. At that time, private prison corporations had lined up for the profits, charging much more to house women with children than single adults. Now the race was on to care for children by themselves, and it came at a huge price to the federal government. Not only was housing thousands of children separated from their parents expensive, taxpayers would also bear the cost of prosecuting all the adults charged with felonies for crossing the border. Public pressure escalated, and on June 20, 2018, just a few months after the policy's implementation, Trump signed an executive order rescinding the separation of children from their parents. But thousands had already been separated. Trump had previously said that he had just been following settled law and only Congress could stop the separation of children from their parents, but with one stroke of the pen, the practice ceased— although Jeff Sessions vowed on the same day, "The President has made clear: we are going to continue to prosecute those adults who enter here illegally."[26]

Trump's most notable immigration reform idea is the building of his "big, beautiful wall."[27] As I've been reporting, the wall and border security infrastructure along the US-Mexico border has been the number one factor in a massive death toll that continues to this day. Trump's wall would extend the existing border walls and fencing from seven hundred miles to nearly two thousand, and he wants to reinforce the existing infrastructure. Democratic staff on the Senate Homeland Security and Governmental Affairs Committee believe that this could cost up $66.9 billion, with an annual maintenance fee upward of $150 million.[28]

Even if Trump were to get congressional approval to build the promised wall—and the budget, which is still his biggest hurdle—the logistics are nearly impossible. The terrain along the border is some of the harshest in the country. Years of construction would be necessary just to get ready to build a wall. Mountains and deserts pose construction and maintenance nightmares, and just gaining access to the region is difficult enough. Most of the US border with Mexico sits on hundreds of miles far from any city, and there are often no roads. Those would need to go in first, as well as roads for patrolling and maintaining the structure.

Then there is the business of acquiring land. Texas, for example, is divided from Mexico by the Rio Grande River, a natural border. To build a wall in Texas along the Rio Grande, about five hundred feet of US land would have to be ceded to the other side of the fence. Since the state of Texas allows private citizens to own land right up to the banks of the Rio Grande, the United States would have to purchase almost five thousand parcels of it before it could build anything.[29] Although the Secure Fence Act of 2006 allowed the Bush administration to build more border barriers in strategic regions along the Rio Grande, it had a hard time acquiring the private land. Over three hundred lawsuits were filed against the government's encroachment. In fact, as of 2019, thirteen years later, more than eighty of the original lawsuits are still in litigation.[30]

So far, there has been no viable plan to build the wall—at least any plan available to the public—nor is there enough political will to move Trump's signature border security idea forward, especially as Democrats control the House as of 2019. In December 2018, Trump threatened to shut down the government if he did not receive at least $5 billion to begin construction of his border wall. He made good on his promise, refusing to sign a measure to keep the government open unless it included his $5 billion for border wall construction. What resulted was the longest government shutdown in US history—thirty-five days and just a little over a billion dollars in appropriations to strengthen the current border wall and add a few more miles to it.[31] Four companies won bids to build prototypes, but the administration has not yet chosen one.[32] Trump's grand idea has also changed over time. Initially, he said that the entire border needed to be walled off, then maybe a thousand miles of it, and now maybe only seven hundred more miles is sufficient.[33] It appears that Trump's border wall has little basis in reality. His original idea of building a "big, beautiful wall" has given way to more recent admissions that parts of the border may never be walled off. Congress has no bill to vote on for a border wall, there are no known plans of what the wall would look like border-wide, and certainly, no money is coming from Mexico to build it. It appears that Trump just needs to keep his wall idea alive to feed his political base. At campaign rallies, every time he brings up the wall, his audience cheers wildly at it despite the idea being locked in limbo.

Even without the wall, Trump's policies and executive orders since January 2017 have made crossing the border deadlier, and life in the United States for undocumented immigrants is even more precarious. None of this has altered the flow of migration, though it has trended down steadily since 2000 and is at its lowest in four decades.[34] Yet the number of migrants who have died in the American Southwest deserts and in detention centers is on the rise. It is difficult to make any hard determination about border security efficacy from federal statistics, but one point seems to be evident: there have been fewer apprehensions, suggesting that fewer people are crossing the border illegally—at least, that is how the government sees it. If this is true, then the increase in the number of migrant bodies suggests that the death rate continues to climb. For example, in 2017, migrant deaths were up as much as 55 percent in some regions of Arizona while overall apprehensions were at a record low.[35] Most likely, crossing the border has become increasingly dangerous.

- - -

Still, none of Trump's border policies will dissuade migrants from coming.

Telma, a single mother, came to the US-Mexico border from Suchitepequez in Guatemala because she had no other choice. Local gangs had threatened her twelve-year-old daughter, pressuring her to become a gang banger. If she had joined, the young girl would probably have been raped as a form of initiation, and she would have been tattooed with gang insignia. She would have been forced to do drugs like the rest of the young gang members and then probably to commit some form of petty theft to prove that she had what it took. If she refused any of this, she would most likely have been bullied every day on her way to school and back. If she could resist the taunts, she would most likely have been beaten. If she still resisted, she would likely have been killed.

Telma's daughter's story is not uncommon for youth in Central America. The gangs recruit the young and push them into a world of drugs and crime before they even know what they are doing. Telma was aware that her daughter could fall victim to gang indoctrination any day, and she needed to protect her from it. The gangs had killed her husband the year before because he had refused to pay extortion money. As a woman alone in Guatemala, it was tough enough to try to make ends meet, let alone protect her daughter from the growing influence of the gangs. She had heard that the United States would accept requests for asylum from gang violence, so she knew she had to make the journey northward. She had never been to the United States and had no relatives there. The only thing on her mind was the need to protect her daughter, so she packed up what little she had and made her way.

Telma and her daughter rode a few buses for more than a thousand miles to the port of entry in Nogales, Mexico—just south of the border from Nogales, Arizona. She had heard that migrants could ask a US border official for asylum at any port of entry. She was aware that her chances having it granted were slim. In fact, during the Obama administration, over 80 percent of asylum claims had been rejected.[36] Still, a slim chance was better than staying in Guatemala.

By the time Telma and her daughter arrived in Nogales, they had been on the road for two weeks. They had no money for hotels or food, so they had stopped at a few migrant shelters along the way. They also could not pay full fare to the border, so they borrowed money wherever they could. When they arrived at the port of entry, Telma thought, *We each made it in one piece.* Maybe now there was reason for hope. Maybe now her daughter could be safe. What she hadn't expected was the long line at the border. She and her daughter were only two among thousands of other refugees waiting to make claims.

Telma hadn't realized that, several months before she and her daughter had left for the border, the Trump administration had made the process of claiming asylum more difficult. Until recently, those claiming asylum could speak to US officials and be processed immediately. For some reason, there was a wait now even to see an official, and it got longer as asylum seekers kept coming. When Telma arrived, she heard that it could be more than two weeks. The wait as of early 2019 was several months. CBP told me that the slowdown was because

> the number of inadmissible individuals CBP is able to process varies based upon case complexity; available resources; medical needs; translation requirements; holding/detention space; overall port volume; and ongoing enforcement actions. No one is being denied the opportunity to make a claim of credible fear or seek asylum. CBP officers allow more people into our facilities for processing once space becomes available or other factors allow for additional parties to arrive. Depending upon port circumstances at the time of arrival, individuals presenting without documents may need to wait in Mexico as CBP officers work to process those already within our facilities. We expect that this will be a temporary situation.

CBP could not provide me any proof that there was no space or that detention areas were full. In the previous year, 2016, there had been more claims of asylum, and there were no migrants like Telma lining up at the border and waiting. Experts I spoke to had never heard of a wait time just to fill out an application for asylum; the current situation was unprecedented. At the same time, the rules for asylum had become stricter. While Telma and her daughter were traveling to the United States, Jeff Sessions, then attorney general, issued a ruling narrowing the scope of claims that the country would process, directly affecting migrants from Central America like Telma: "Generally, claims by aliens pertaining to domestic violence or gang violence perpetrated by non-governmental actors will not qualify for asylum," wrote Sessions.[37] Such claims had been honored prior to the ruling. Telma's chances to save her daughter had just gotten slimmer.

After Telma's two-week (or longer) wait just to make a claim, the process itself could take months after that—and even then, there was no guarantee of asylum. Where would she wait? She had no money and no place to stay. When I met her, she was sitting in the sweltering heat on a sidewalk that leads up to the port of entry with other migrants and their children. If she had to wait two weeks or two years to make a claim of asylum, she would. She would not be heading back home. She had come all this way and was without options. She would try her best to provide a safe home for her daughter.

Given all the obstacles Telma had overcome and survived just to be at the doorstep of the United States was enough to strengthen her resolve. She eventually got in to file her claim, but I am not sure if her request was ever granted. She and her daughter were lost to the maze of detention facilities. They might have been deported because the threats they had faced no longer qualified them to seek safety here. At that time, the Trump administration denial rates for asylum seekers jumped by 89 percent, meaning that more asylum seekers would be denied their requests and sent back to their countries of origin.[38]

- - -

In October 2018, about ten thousand migrants, mostly from Honduras, organized into what is now known as the migrant caravan. The group formed as a response to the violence, poverty, and drought that had stricken its region and made living there nearly impossible. For many years prior, Central American migrants had suffered extortion, kidnapping, robbery, and rape as they made their journey through Mexico to the US border. The idea of the caravan was to offer people safety in numbers as they left their homes for a better life; they didn't have to pay high cartel fees for protection, and a large caravan was quite visible.

I joined the caravan when it came to Mexico City and made its way to Tijuana, Mexico, just south of San Diego, California—which was its eventual destination. I spoke to dozens of migrants about why they were coming and heard similar stories of violence and poverty that had forced them northward from their own country. Trump had heard of the caravan and declared that "criminals and unknown Middle Easterners are mixed in" among those traveling in the caravan.[39] These statements quickly criminalized the group, and both the right-wing media and the president referred to its members as invaders.

One story that I heard repeatedly from Central American migrants surprised me. A prolonged drought in their regions had persisted for about five years, and this year had been especially harsh. I traveled to the "dry corridor" of Central America where the drought had hit hardest due to climate change—parts of Guatemala, El Salvador, and Honduras. Migrants told me that the rains would come, and staple crops like corn and beans would sprout, but then the rains would stop and the crops would dry well before harvest, leaving the farmers with almost complete crop failure.

The drought had persisted for long enough that the World Food Programme (WFP) of the United Nations had set up offices there. People were starving. When I visited in late 2018, the WFP had already declared that four hundred thousand people in the region had reached famine status.[40] It was difficult to determine exactly how many people in the caravan were leaving because of famine, but all of the hundreds I spoke to, in particular Hondurans, had been somewhat affected. Many had been farmers who had lost their crops of corn, beans, rice, or bananas. They had sold farming tools, and some had sold their land if they could and tried to get jobs in nearby towns, but those were scarce or paid poorly. I spoke to farmers who said they had been living on one tortilla a day—that's why they joined the caravan. Lori Melo of the WFP in Guatemala told me that over half of farmers who had lost their crops were choosing to migrate, many to Mexico or eventually to the US.

I looked for statements from the Trump administration about the drought in Central America and support for the crisis of famine that was sure to worsen if the drought persisted, but I could find no acknowledgement of climate change or recognition of famine in the region. The WFP declares that by 2019, over two million people will go hungry there, and that number is expected to climb if conditions remain the same.[41] If millions of Central Americans go hungry next year and in years to come, how many will be forced to flee north?

The ten thousand migrants who began the caravan in Central America had dwindled by half by the time it reached the US-Mexico border. They encountered five thousand National Guard troops courtesy of the Trump administration, along with concertina wire added to border fences and tear gas shot across the border. How will future waves of migrants be greeted as they seek refuge, especially if millions come? The Trump administration's "seal the border" approach is unlikely to stem the flow of migrants trying to cross in the coming years. And given the administration's refusal to acknowledge the effects of climate change, I doubt that it will institute policies to offset the devastation wrought by famine and drought. So far, the administration has not acknowledged a climate crisis in Central America as the impetus of the caravan or other waves of migration, ignoring the precedent set by the United Nations, which described it in "Food Security and Emigration," a report published in 2017 detailing the effects of prolonged drought in the region and the factors that force people to flee their homeland.[42]

Conclusion

The United States acquired the territory along the southwestern border through war. Texas had been the product of a land grab, and the famous battle at the Alamo was over what was known to be Mexico's sovereign land. The United States acquired New Mexico, Arizona, Colorado, and California through a bloody conflict that ended in 1848, culminating in the country's payment of $15 million in damages. And this is how the current border between the United States and Mexico was formed.

Since then, and increasingly since the 1980s, that border has been militarized—all in an effort to keep out migrants. The region has become, for all intents and purposes, a war zone, although Congress has formally declared nothing of the kind.

Starting with the formation of the Border Patrol almost a hundred years ago, the country has added more security infrastructure rather than taking it away. The United States has added more defense contractors, more machinery, more walls, and more troops with more guns. The National Guard deploys to the border any time the president deems it necessary. Drones fly over the thin line that separates the two countries. Black Hawk helicopters patrol US citizens' backyards along the border. Federally manned checkpoints stop all vehicles near the border. Immigration and Customs Enforcement (ICE) conducts regular raids targeting undocumented immigrants in cities and towns across the country.

The United States has invested billions—and with Donald Trump as president and obsessed with building a wall, that number will only increase—to defend itself from men, women, and children from Mexico and Central America seeking jobs and better lives. In spite of the buildup and investments, there is still no metric that truly determines whether the border security strategy is even effective. Based on what I've observed and reported, migrants keep coming. In 2018, there were nearly four hundred thousand apprehensions at the US-Mexico border.[1] Although that number is at historic lows for migration, it still constitutes a large mass of humanity. Neither walls, border guards, the threat of incarceration, family separation, nor death have stopped the influx. They keep coming because the push factors associated with migration have not been resolved. Poverty, violence, and now climate change make living conditions in Mexico and Central America too dangerous and difficult for survival. All the United States needs for apprehensions to spike is an economic recession in Mexico or a civil war in El Salvador. Such factors have created migration spikes in the past, and they most likely will again. Militarization of the border can only make migration more difficult and dangerous. Without any remedy for the reasons that people come, they will continue.

It is difficult to determine whether the war on migrants at the border is an artifact of politicians trying to scare constituents into voting for them or defense contractors lobbying to create a new market for their goods when opportunities abroad dry up. Certainly, for the past few decades, policy makers have failed to pass meaningful legislative solutions to alleviate the backlog of immigration requests or of domestic demand for labor. There has been no amnesty for the undocumented population that remains in the shadows. Instead, the response has been to tighten the screws, making it harder for people to come legally—sometimes with deadly consequences.

I continue to be puzzled by the war at the US-Mexico border and the continued buildup of security infrastructure. I have spoken to many politicians and leaders who believe that the current system of security is ineffective at best. They are aware that we must reform the US immigration system wholesale. The implementers of border militarization back in the 1980s and 1990s agreed that just adding Border Patrol agents and fences would not resolve illegal immigration; for an effective strategy, we also had to address why people come and go. So many decision makers know the facts, but so few seem to take the lead on meaningful reform.

If we spend billions of dollars to fortify the border, what about using them to help stabilize the economies of Central America and Mexico? What about focusing efforts on legal worker programs to bring those who are looking for work safely to jobs in the United States instead of forcing them through a death maze in the desert? What about staffing immigration courts to clear the two-year backlog of cases so that people don't languish in detention? Maybe these aren't platforms that politicians are willing to run on. Maybe it's easier to scare people by saying that terrorists are coming to the country and that building a wall will save them. I suppose it's more difficult to "unscare" people than it is to find reasonable approaches.

Maybe it's more primal than that. Maybe many Americans don't like the idea of more Latinos in the United States. Maybe they prefer a whiter society. I find it difficult to believe that racism and xenophobia alone have caused the massive militarization of the US-Mexico border, but it's also difficult to refute that it has played an integral part. The idea of immigration reform and granting rights to foreigners can bring out the worst in people. Immigrants are easy to scapegoat, and foreigners are easy to misunderstand. Politicians find it difficult to run on nuance when a topic is so complex. All these factors, and probably many more, create a difficult arena for reform.

If I were to boil the problem down to one simple concept, I would echo Martin Luther King Jr., who once stated, "Nothing in the world is more dangerous than sincere ignorance and conscientious stupidity."[2]

I know immigrants; I know undocumented immigrants. I have met thousands of people on the journey to the United States from Latin America, and I have never felt threatened or fearful. I have met some of the kindest, most entrepreneurial, smartest, and humblest of people. The spirit of a person who is unwilling to settle for the meager offerings that a corrupt government like that of Honduras has to offer and risks his or her life to feed a family is powerfully inspiring to me. The United States benefits from such resiliency and resolve. It sounds like an ethereal idea and certainly is not a great basis for a political stump speech, but maybe if we knew migrants better, we would be less willing to separate their families or endanger their lives. But, of course, fearmongering, misinformation, and ignorance seem to rule the debate today, and as long as US residents remain afraid of immigrants, border security will most likely be the antidote.

- - -

I remember the first time I saw the bodies of migrants in the California desert.

It was 2006, and I had been documenting the search efforts of a nonprofit group known as Angels of the Desert. They had a missing persons report for a pair of cousins, both in their twenties, who had been deported after a city cop had cited them for a faulty taillight. The two men had had no legal papers when the cop pulled them over, but they had lived in the United States for over a decade. Both had US citizen children, yet there was still no legal way for them to plead their cases and remain in the country with their families. They planned to return illegally.

They had let their families know of the plan, which meant a trek through the vast California desert. They had figured the trip would take them a few days, as they were both young and healthy and had plenty of water. They had assured their families that they would be careful. But after two days, the families lost contact with the men. A week went by, and still no word. No one was sure what happened.

The Angels of the Desert search and rescue team knew where to start looking, and within a few hours, we found their bodies lying next to each other under a small shrub. It was 118 degrees that day. The men had been dead for about five days, yet already their faces were gone. Animals and insects eat the soft tissues of the face first. They still had their clothes on. Two one-gallon water bottles lay nearby. One had urine in it, and the other was empty. It is clear that the men had run out of water and began to drink their own urine to survive.

I was stunned to see two bodies killed by the desert, lying in the middle of nowhere. The shock of that horrible sight has never left me and returns every time I encounter similar scenes, over and over. I can't help but ask why the United States would create policies that lead to these kinds of deaths. The only reason that the two had risked their lives was that they wanted to see their children grow to adulthood. They wanted to kiss their wives. They wanted to return to their jobs and lives and futures. They had been deemed criminals because they had crossed the border; they had lost their lives because they had been forced into the hot desert as their only route of return.

I am a journalist and have taken care to tell these stories without bias. But when I witness such horrors, I wonder when we, as a country and a society, will finally acknowledge that this is wrong. Not only that, but that US policy is directly responsible for migrant deaths in hot deserts or in detention centers, for children being separated from their parents, for families being divided forever—and for continuing to close the door tighter and tighter to our poor and desperate neighbors. We all admit that it was wrong to enslave Africans, slaughter Native Americans, intern Japanese Americans, forbid women the right to vote, deny interracial and same-sex marriage, and undermine civil rights. I am not sure if we are at the point where we can acknowledge that the way that the United States manages its borders and the way it wages war against immigrants is wrong. I fear that more will be denied access to the United States, more will attempt to enter illegally, and more will die—possibly for years to come. I hope the problem is resolved more quickly than I expect. Until then, I will continue to report on this topic until I can file my last piece, knowing that it has become part of our dark, stained history.

Acknowledgments

It would be impossible to acknowledge and express the correct amount of gratitude to all those who contributed to the pages of this book. Every immigrant, border official, politician, expert, publication, and broadcast outlet has had a direct hand in helping to tell the stories I have been fortunate enough to report over the past many years. But there are those who deserve my indebtedness and acknowledgment because without their expertise and care, reporting at the border and turning it into a book would never have been possible. Thank you to Esther Kaplan, editor-in-chief at Type Investigations at the Type Media Center, who spent many days of her life over seeing my reporting. Her expert eye shaped the stories and her passion for great reporting pushed me to keep digging. It is a small sentiment of praise to state that that many of the stories in this book would never have been reported if it hadn't been for her dedication to the field of investigative reporting. She has made me the reporter I am today. In addition, Taya Kitman at Type Media Center deserves my gratitude for keeping the funding alive, necessary to tell the kinds of stories few are willing to invest in.

I would like to thank Katy O'Donnell, senior editor at Bold Type Books, for encouraging the subject matter and helping to turn my broadcast stories into something people would actually want to read. She has guided the entire process of taking years of reporting and turning them into a book. Thank you to Darren Ankrom, who made sure the facts in the book are accurate, and Megan Schindele, who made the process of publishing a book smooth and organized. Many stories remain untold because there are too few advocates like Clive Priddle, publisher at Bold Type Books at Hachette, who said yes to making a book about militarization at the US-Mexico border. Thanks also to Brooke Parsons, publicity manager at Bold Type Books, who was willing to work hard to get the word out.

I am also indebted to my family of three sisters, Emma, Ruth, and Eva, who continue to live along the border region of California and frequently tell me stories of this unique part of America. I would also like to thank fondly Jack Lorenz for supporting my goals, dreams, reporting, and well-being for decades. There are too many reporting partners, fellow journalists, and confidants who have helped me along the way, but a few have affected my life profoundly: Brian Epstein, John Larson, Thomas Backer, Solly Granatstein, Lucian Read, Hannah Rappleye, James Blue, Brian Ross, Rhonda Schwartz, Spencer Wilking, Adam Giese, Dan Rather, Will Carless, Greg Gilderman, Neil Katz, Shawn Efran, Adam Yamaguchi, Katie Arnoldi, Alice Brennan, Kim Cookson, Joe Cutbirth, Michael Fritz, Stephen Fee, Marc Rosenwasser, Enrique Acevedo, and Marisa Venegas.

Most importantly, I would like to express my gratitude to all those who, in the face of suffering, discrimination, rejection, fear, persecution, injustice, and even death, have been willing to share their stories and lives with me in the most public of ways. I have a better understanding of life and its struggles thanks to those I have been fortunate to report about, and I am forever grateful for their candid generosity.

Notes

Chapter 1: Seeds of War

1 Benjamin Franklin, *Letter to Peter Collinson*, Teaching AmericanHistory.org, February 25, 2019, http://teachingameri canhistory.org/library/document/letter-to-peter-collinson/.

2 "Border Patrol History," US Customs and Border Protection, last modified October 5, 2018, https://www.cbp.gov/border -security/along-us-borders/history.

3 "Border Patrol History," US Customs and Border Protection.

4 Kelly Lytle Hernandez, *Migra!: A History of the U.S. Border Patrol* (Berkeley: University of California Press, 2010), 27.

5 Robert D. Schroeder, "Holding the Line in the 21st Century," November 25, 2014, https://www.cbp.gov/sites/default/files /documents/Holding%20the%20Line_TRILOGY.pdf, 14.

6 Hernandez, *Migra!*, 29.

7 "The Immigration Act of 1924," US Department of State, Office of the Historian, Last modified November 18, 2018, https:// history.state.gov/milestones/1921-1936/immigration-act.

8 US House of Representatives Art and History Archive, "The Immigration Act of 1924," February 18, 2009, https://history.house.gov/Historical-Highlights/1901-1950/The-Immigration-Act-of-1924/.

9 "Recognizing the Seventy-Five Years of Service," House of Representatives Congressional Record, November 10, 1999, https://www.congress.gov/congressional-record/1999/11/10/house-section/article/H11922-1.

10 Deborah Waller Meyers, "From Horseback to High Tech: US Border Enforcement," Migration Policy Institute, February 1, 2006, https://www.migrationpolicy.org/article/horseback-high-tech-us-border-enforcement.

11 Maclovio Perez Jr., Texas State Historical Association, "El Paso Bath Riots," February 18, 2019, https://ftp.tshaonline.org/handbook/online/articles/jce02.

12 United States Public Health Service, *Public Health Reports, Volume 32, Part 1*, January–June 1917 (Washington, DC: Government Printing Office, 1918), accessed via https://books.google.com/books?id=WE8yAQAAMAAJ.

13 "The Refusal of Carmelita Torres," Latino Rebels, September 27, 2015, https://www.latinorebels.com/2015/09/27/the-refusal-of-carmelita-torres/.

14 David Dorado Romo, *Ringside Seat to a Revolution* (El Paso, TX: Cinco Puntos Press), 223.

15 John Burnett, "The Bath Riots: Indignity Along the Mexican Border," *NPR Weekend Edition*, January 26, 2006, https://www.npr.org/templates/story/story.php?storyId=5176177.

16 "Border Patrol History," US Customs and Border Protection.

17 "Audio Interview with Carranco Flores," Bracero History Archive, January 2, 2019, http://braceroarchive.org/archive/files/carrancofuentes_96e8db7ab6.mp3.

18 Robert Pear, "Congress Winding Up Work, Votes Sweeping Aliens Bill; Reagan Expected to Sign It," *New York Times*, October 18, 1986, https://www.nytimes.com/1986/10/18/us

/congress-winding-up-work-votes-sweeping-aliens-bill-reagan
-expected-to-sign-it.html.

19 Pia M. Orrenius and Madeline Zavodny, "Do Amnesty Programs Reduce Undocumented Immigration? Evidence from IRCA," *Demography* 40, no. 3 (August 2003): 437–450.

20 "Stats and Summaries," US Customs and Border Protection, December 12, 2018, https://www.cbp.gov/newsroom/media
-resources/stats.

21 "National Trends," TRAC Immigration, November 18, 2018, https://trac.syr.edu/immigration/reports/143/include/rep143
table3.html.

22 Joshua Linder, "The Amnesty Effect: Evidence from the 1986 Immigration Reform and Control Act," *The Public Purpose*, November 2, 2018, https://www.american.edu/spa
/publicpurpose/upload/2011-public-purpose-amnesty-effect
.pdf.

23 Pear, "Congress Winding Up Work."

24 "Kae T. Patrick," Revolvy.com, accessed March 5, 2019, https://www.revolvy.com/page/Kae-T.-Patrick.

25 Raymond Tatalovich, *Nativism Reborn?: The Official English Language Movement and the American States* (Lexington: University Press of Kentucky), 266.

26 Annelise Anderson, *Illegal Aliens and Employer Sanctions: Solving the Wrong Problem,* in *Hoover Essays in Public Policy* (Stanford, CA: Hoover Institution, 1986), 27.

27 Cathleen Decker and Daniel M. Weintraub, "Wilson Savors Win; Democrats Assess Damage." *Los Angeles Times*, November 10, 1994, http://articles.latimes.com/1994-11-10
/news/mn-61016_1_democratic-party.

28 Elson Trinidad, *Proposition 187 Passes; Sparks Immigration Debate,* KCET, September 2, 2014, https://www.kcet.org
/kcet-50th-anniversary/november-1994-proposition-187-passes
-sparks-immigration-debate.

29 Decker and Weintraub, "Wilson Savors Win."

30 Nancy H. Martis, "#187 Illegal Immigrants. Ineligibility for Public Services. Verification and Reporting," California Voter Foundation, 1994, https://archive.calvoter.org/archive /94general/props/187.html.

31 Decker and Weintraub, "Wilson Savors Win."

32 Mark Z. Barabak, "Pete Wilson Looks Back on Proposition 187," *Los Angeles Times*, March 23, 2017, https://www .latimes.com/politics/la-me-on-politics-column-20170323 -story.html.

33 Gebe Martinez, "Learning from Proposition 187," Center for American Progress, May 5, 2010, https://www.americanpro gress.org/issues/immigration/news/2010/05/05/7847/learning -from-proposition-187/.

34 Raoul Lowery Contreras, *The New American Majority* (Lincoln, NE: Writer's Showcase iUniverse Inc.), 128.

35 Matt Barreto, "The Prop 187 Effect: How the California GOP Lost Their Way and Implications for 2014 and Beyond," *Latino Decisions*, October 17, 2013, http://www.latinodecisions .com/blog/2013/10/17/prop187effect/.

Chapter 2: The War Begins—Again

1 Wayne Cornelius, "Evaluating Enhanced US Border Enforcement," Migration Policy Institute, May 1, 2004, http:// www.migrationpolicy.org/article/evaluating-enhanced-us -border-enforcement.

2 Josue Gonzalez, "What We Learned from NAFTA," *New York Times*, November 24, 2013, https://www.nytimes.com /roomfordebate/2013/11/24/what-weve-learned-from-nafta.

3 Paola Pereznieto, "The Case of Mexico's 1995 Peso Crisis and Argentina's 2002 Convertibility Crisis: Including Children in Policy Responses to Previous Economic Crises," UNICEF, accessed July 27, 2014, https://www.unicef.org /socialpolicy/files/Impact_of_Econ_Shocks_Mexico_and _Argentina(3).pdf.

4 Ana Gonzalez Barrera and Jens Manuel Krogstad, "What We Know About Illegal Immigration from Mexico," Pew Research Center, December 3, 2018, http://www.pewre search.org/fact-tank/2018/12/03/what-we-know-about-illegal -immigration-from-mexico/.

5 Seth Mydans, "One Last Deadly Crossing for Illegal Aliens," *New York Times,* January 7, 1991, https://www.nytimes .com/1991/01/07/us/one-last-deadly-crossing-for-illegal-aliens .html.

6 Monica Rodriguez, "Caltrans to Build I-5 Safety Fence," *Los Angeles Times,* December 20, 1990, http://articles.latimes .com/1990-12-20/local/me-9164_1_camp-pendleton.

7 National Drug Control Strategy, The White House, January 1992, https://www.ncjrs.gov/pdffiles1/ondcp/134372.pdf.

8 Michael Coleman, "Feds Fine Sandia for Improper Lobbying," *Albuquerque Journal,* August 24, 2015, https://www .abqjournal.com/633395/sandia-corp-pays-4-8-million-fine -for-improper-lobbying.html.

9 "CBP's Border Security Efforts—An Analysis of the Southwest Border Security Between Ports of Entry," Department of Homeland Security, Oversight.gov, February 27, 2017, https://www.oversight.gov/sites/default/files/oig-reports/OIG -17-39-Feb17.pdf.

10 Olivia Mena, "A Comparative Political Sociology of Contemporary National Border Barriers" (PhD diss., London School of Economics and Political Science, September 2015), http:// etheses.lse.ac.uk/3281/1/Doerge_Nomos.pdf.

11 "CBP's Border Security Efforts," Department of Homeland Security, February 27, 2017 https://www.oversight.gov/sites /default/files/oig-reports/OIG-17-39-Feb17.pdf.

12 Adriana Pinon, "Your Rights in the Border Zone," ACLU, February 13, 2018, https://www.aclu.org/blog/immigrants-rights /immigrants-rights-and-detention/your-rights-border-zone.

13 "CBP's Border Security Efforts," Department of Homeland Security.

14 "Federation for Immigration Reform," Southern Poverty Law Center, December 16, 2018, https://www.splcenter.org /fighting-hate/extremist-files/group/federation-american -immigration-reform.

15 Tom Barry, "'Border Control' Before 'Border Security,'" *Border Lines* (blog), March 24, 2011, http://borderlinesblog.blog spot.com/2011/03/border-control-before-border-security.html.

16 Doris Meissner Interview with John Carlos Frey, August 2007.

17 "Border Patrol Strategic Plan 1994 and Beyond," US Border Patrol, Homeland Security Digital Library, July 1994, https:// www.hsdl.org/?abstract&did=721845.

18 "US Border Patrol Fiscal Year Staffing Statistics (FY 1992– 2017)," US Customs and Border Protection, December 12, 2017, https://www.cbp.gov/document/stats/us-border-patrol -fiscal-year-staffing-statistics-fy-1992-fy-2017.

19 "Border Patrol Strategic Plan 1994 and Beyond," US Border Patrol.

20 "Border Patrol Strategic Plan 1994 and Beyond," US Border Patrol.

21 James Bornemeier, "El Paso Plan Deters Illegal Immigrants," *Los Angeles Times*, July 27, 1994, http://articles.latimes.com /1994-07-27/news/mn-20325_1_el-paso.

22 Timothy J. Dunn and José Palafox, "Militarization of the Border," *Jose Palafox* (blog), November 13, 2013, https://jose palafox.wordpress.com/2013/11/13/militarization-of-the-border -by-timothy-j-dunn-jose-palafox-2005/.

23 "United States Border Patrol Southwest Border Sectors," US Customs and Border Protection, September 30, 2017, https:// www.cbp.gov/sites/default/files/assets/documents/2017 -Dec/BP%20Southwest%20Border%20Sector%20Apps%20 FY1960%20-%20FY2017.pdf.

24 "US Border Patrol's Implementation of 'Operation Gate-keeper,'" Homeland Security Digital Library, August 9, 1996, https://www.hsdl.org/?abstract&did=464221.

25 "Border Control," US General Accounting Office, March 10, 1995, https://www.gao.gov/assets/110/105884.pdf.

26 "Illegal Immigration: Immigration Border-Crossing: Deaths Have Doubled Since 1995," US Government Accountability Office, August 15, 2006, https://www.gao.gov/products/GAO-06-770.

27 Wayne Cornelius and Claudia E. Smith, "Putting People in Harm's Way," *Los Angeles Times,* September 21, 1998, http://articles.latimes.com/1998/sep/21/local/me-24993.

28 Dunn and Palafox, "Militarization."

29 Dunn and Palafox, "Militarization."

30 Doris Meissner, "Illegal Immigration Pressures," *Migration News,* May 1995, https://migration.ucdavis.edu/mn/more.php?id=630.

31 "US Border Patrol's Implementation," Homeland Security Digital Library.

32 Duncan Hunter Interview with John Carlos Frey, August 2007.

33 Dr. John Hunter, *The Space Show*, February 25, 2018, https://www.thespaceshow.com/guest/dr.-john-hunter.

34 "US Border Patrol Fiscal Year Staffing Statistics," US Customs and Border Protection.

35 "US Border Patrol's Implementation," Homeland Security Digital Library.

36 Dunn and Palafox, "Militarization."

37 "US Border Patrol's Implementation," Homeland Security Digital Library.

38 "Total Illegal Alien Apprehension by Fiscal Year," United States Border Patrol, April 11, 2013, https://www.hsdl.org/?view&did=734433.

39 "Flashback: Democrats Talk Tough on Immigration," GOP.com, January 25, 2018, https://gop.com/flashback-democrats-talked-tough-on-immigration-rsr/.

40 "1995 State of the Union Address," *Washington Post*, January 24, 1995, https://www.washingtonpost.com/wp-srv/politics/special/states/docs/sou95.htm.

41 "The Personal Responsibility and Work Opportunity Reconciliation Act of 1996," Office of the Assistant Secretary for Planning and Evaluation, September 1, 1996, https://aspe.hhs .gov/report/personal-responsibility-and-work-opportunity-rec onciliation-act-1996.

42 Audrey Singer, "Welfare Reform and Immigrants," Brookings, May 1, 2004, https://www.brookings.edu/research/welfare -reform-and-immigrants/.

43 "Analysis of Immigration Detention Policies," American Civil Liberties Union, October 12, 2018, https://www.aclu.org /other/analysis-immigration-detention-policies.

44 "104th Congress Public Law 208," US Government Printing Office, September 30, 1997, https://www.gpo.gov/fdsys/pkg /PLAW-104publ208/html/PLAW-104publ208.htm.

45 Eric Schmitt, "Milestones and Missteps on Immigration," *New York Times*, October 26, 1996, https://www.nytimes .com/1996/10/26/us/milestones-and-missteps-on-immigration .html.

46 "Delegation of Immigration Authority Section 287(g) Immigration and Nationality Act," US Immigration and Customs Enforcement, August 10, 2018, https://www.ice.gov/287g.

47 Zenen Jaimes Perez, "Removing Barriers to Higher Education for Undocumented Students," Center for American Progress, December 5, 2014, https://www.americanprogress.org /issues/immigration/reports/2014/12/05/101366/removing-bar riers-to-higher-education-for-undocumented-students/.

Chapter 3: The Military Arrives at the Border

1 Monte Paulsen, "Fatal Error Hooked on Drug Money," *Austin Chronicle*, December 25, 1998, https://www.austinchron icle.com/news/1998-12-25/520877/.

2 "Investigation to Inquire in the Circumstances Surrounding the Joint Task Force-6 (JTF-6) Shooting Incident That Occurred on 20 May 1997 Near the Border Between the

United States and Mexico, United States," US Marine Corps Report, Drug Policy Forum of Texas, April 7, 1998, http://www.dpft.org/hernandez/coyne.htm.

3 "The Posse Comitatus Act and Related Matters: The Use of the Military to Execute Civilian Law," EveryCRSReport. com, June 1, 2000, https://www.everycrsreport.com/reports /95-964.html.

4 "The Posse Comitatus Act," EveryCRSReport.com.

5 "The Posse Comitatus Act," EveryCRSReport.com.

6 "Military Support for Civilian Law Enforcement Agencies," USCode.House.gov, September 12, 2018, http://uscode.house .gov/view.xhtml?path=/prelim@title10/subtitleA/part1/chap ter15&edition=prelim.

7 Paulsen, "Fatal Error."

8 "H.Con.Res.274—Reaffirming the continued importance and applicability of the Posse Comitatus Act," Congress.gov, October 16, 2018, https://www.congress.gov/bill/109th-congress /house-concurrent-resolution/274.

9 Robert Longley, "Posse Comitatus Act and the US Military on the Border," *ThoughtCo.*, April 8, 2018, https://www.thoughtco .com/posse-comitatus-act-military-on-border-3321286.

10 Frederick Turner and Bryanna Fox, *Police Militarization: Policy Changes and Stakeholders' Opinions in the United States*, SpringerBriefs in Criminology (Cham, Switzerland: Springer), 2018.

11 Timothy J. Dunn and José Palafox, "Militarization of the Border," *Jose Palafox* (blog), November 13, 2013, https://jose palafox.wordpress.com/2013/11/13/militarization-of-the-border -by-timothy-j-dunn-jose-palafox-2005/.

12 Paulsen, "Fatal Error."

13 Robert Draper, "Soldiers of Misfortune," *Texas Monthly*, August 1997, https://www.texasmonthly.com/articles/soldiers -of-misfortune-2/.

14 "National Drug Control Strategy," The White House, September 5, 1989, available at National Criminal Justice Reference Service, https://www.ncjrs.gov/pdffiles1/ondcp/119466.pdf.

15 Paulsen, "Fatal Error."

16 Josiah Heyman and Howard Campbell, "The Militarization of the United States-Mexico Border Region," University of Texas, El Paso, April 27, 2012, https://www.researchgate.net /publication/259892788_The_Militarization_of_the_United _States-_Mexico_Border_Region.

17 "Law of War / Introduction to Rules of Engagement," US Marine Corps, Basic School, March 12, 2018, https://www .trngcmd.marines.mil/Portals/207/Docs/TBS/B130936%20 Law%20of%20War%20and%20Rules%20Of%20Engage ment.pdf.

18 "Law of War / Introduction to Rules of Engagement," US Marine Corps.

19 Heyman and Campbell, "Militarization."

20 "Investigation," US Marine Corps Report.

21 Heyman and Campbell, "Militarization."

22 Heyman and Campbell, "Militarization."

23 "Investigation," US Marine Corps Report.

24 Heyman and Campbell, "Militarization."

25 "Investigation," US Marine Corps Report.

26 "Investigation," US Marine Corps Report.

27 Paulsen, "Fatal Error."

28 "Investigation," US Marine Corps Report.

29 Draper, "Soldiers of Misfortune."

30 Draper, "Soldiers of Misfortune."

31 Paulsen, "Fatal Error."

32 "Investigation," US Marine Corps Report.

33 "Investigation," US Marine Corps Report.

34 "Investigation," US Marine Corps Report.

35 Sam Howe Verhovek, "After Marine on Patrol Kills a Teen-Ager, a Texas Border Village Wonders Why," *New York Times*, June 29, 1997, https://www.nytimes.com/1997/06/29/us/after -marine-on-patrol-kills-a-teen-ager-a-texas-border-village -wonders-why.html.

36 "Investigation," US Marine Corps Report.

37 "Investigation," US Marine Corps Report.

38 "Investigation," US Marine Corps Report.

39 "CBP Hires Veterans," US Customs and Border Protection, December 21, 2018 https://www.cbp.gov/careers/veterans#militarycommunity_desktop.

Chapter 4: September 11

1 "Border Patrol Overview Mission," US Customs and Border Protection, April 26, 2018, https://www.cbp.gov/border-security/along-us-borders/overview.

2 "National Strategy for Homeland Security," Department of Homeland Security, October 5, 2007, https://www.dhs.gov/xlibrary/assets/nat_strat_homelandsecurity_2007.pdf.

3 Budget in Brief: Fiscal Year 2005," Department of Homeland Security, November 16, 2018, https://www.dhs.gov/xlibrary/assets/FY_2005_BIB_4.pdf.

4 "Border Security: Apprehensions of 'Other Than Mexican' Aliens," CRS Report for Congress, September 22, 2005, https://trac.syr.edu/immigration/library/P1.pdf.

5 "Plugging the Gaps in Border Security," House Hearing Subcommittee on Infrastructure and Border Security, October 16, 2003, https://www.gpo.gov/fdsys/pkg/CHRG-108hhrg21510/html/CHRG-108hhrg21510.htm.

6 "Israeli Technology to Keep Borders Safe," Israel 21c.org, October 5, 2006, https://www.israel21c.org/israeli-technology-to-keep-us-borders-safe/.

7 "Defense: Long Term Contribution Trends," OpenSecrets.org, December 6, 2018, http://www.opensecrets.org/industries/totals.php?cycle=2014&ind=D.

8 "Defense," OpenSecrets.org.

9 "Secure Border Initiative: DHS Has Faced Challenges Deploying Technology and Fencing Along the Southwest Border," US Government Accountability Office, May 4, 2010, https://www.gao.gov/products/GAO-10-651T.

10 "Fallacies of High-Tech Fixes for Border Security," Center for International Policy, April 14, 2010, https://www.inter nationalpolicy.org/research/entry/fallacies-high-tech-fixes -border-security.

11 "Secure Border Initiative," US Government Accountability Office.

12 "Operation Jump Start," National Guard, February 26, 2019, https://www.nationalguard.mil/Resources/Image-Gallery /Historical-Paintings/Heritage-Series/Jump-Start/.

13 "President Bush Signs Secure Fence Act," White House Office of the Press Secretary, October 26, 2006, https:// georgewbushwhitehouse.archives.gov/news/releases/2006 /10/20061026.html.

14 "Vote Passage on Passage of the Bill (H.R. 6061)," US Senate Roll Call, September 29, 2006, https://www.senate .gov/legislative/LIS/roll_call_lists/roll_call_vote_cfm.cfm ?congress=109&session=2&vote=00262#state.

15 "President Bush Signs," White House Office of the Press Secretary.

16 "The Deadly Passage of the All-American Canal," 60 *Minutes*, aired April 30, 2010, https://www.cbsnews.com/news /the-deadly-passage-of-the-all-american-canal/.

17 "The Deadly Passage," 60 *Minutes*.

18 "The Deadly Passage," 60 *Minutes*.

19 "Buoys Strung on Border Canal to Prevent Drownings," Associated Press, November 21, 2015, https://www.foxnews.com /us/buoys-strung-on-border-canal-to-prevent-drownings.

20 Raquel Rubio-Goldsmith et al., "The 'Funnel Effect' & Recovered Bodies of Unauthorized Migrants Processed by the Pima County Office of the Medical Examiner, 1990–2005," SSRN.com, October 2006, https://papers.ssrn.com /sol3/papers.cfm?abstract_id=3040107.

21 Rubio-Goldsmith et al., "The 'Funnel Effect.'"

22 Rubio-Goldsmith et al., "The 'Funnel Effect.'"

23 Lucy Steigerwald, "The Alien Transfer Exit Program Drops Immigrants on the Other Side of the Country," *Hit and*

Run Blog, September 29, 2011, https://reason.com/blog/2011
/09/29/the-alien-transfer-exit-progra.

Chapter 5: Death as Deterrent

1 "Criminal Alien Statistics," US Customs and Border Protection, October 23, 2018, https://www.cbp.gov/newsroom
/stats/cbp-enforcement-statistics/criminal-alien-statistics.

2 "Tucson Sector Arizona," US Customs and Border Protection, December 12, 2018, https://www.cbp.gov/border
-security/along-us-borders/border-patrol-sectors/tucson
-sector-arizona.

3 Brady McCombs and Enric Volante, "Deadliest Migrant
Trail in US," *Arizona Daily Star*, December 9, 2007, https://
tucson.com/news/local/border/deadliest-migrant-trail-in
-u-s-is-right-on-tucson/article_d536fdo4-0718-56ad-af32
-d3480b8b46a6.html.

4 "United States Border Patrol Fiscal Year Southwest Border
Sector Deaths (FY 1998–FY 2017)," US Customs and Border
Protection, last modified December 12, 2017, https://www
.cbp.gov/sites/default/files/assets/documents/2017-Dec
/BP%20Southwest%20Border%20Sector%20Deaths%20
FY1998%20-%20FY2017.pdf.

5 "Remembering the Dead," Coalicion de Derechos Humanos,
January 2, 2019, https://derechoshumanosaz.net/coalition-work
/remembering-the-dead/

6 "A Culture of Cruelty," No More Deaths, 2011, http://forms
.nomoredeaths.org/wp-content/uploads/2014/10/CultureOf
Cruelty-full.compressed.pdf.

7 Jack Lorenz, John Carlos Frey, and Kevin MacLeod, *The
800 Mile Wall* (Gatekeeper Productions, 2009), DVD.

8 "Border Safety Initiative," US Customs and Border Protection, September 9, 2005, https://www.hsdl.org/?view&did
=457099.

9 Carl Prine, "Effective Enforcement Forces Illegal Immigrants onto Tribal Lands, Badlands," Trib Live, July 19, 2015,

https://archive.triblive.com/news/effective-enforcement
-forces-illegal-immigrants-onto-tribal-lands-badlands/.

10 Ned Norris Jr., "Statement from Ned Norris Jr., Chairman,
Tohono O'odham Nation," Official Statement of the Tohono
O'odham Nation, September 2008.

11 "Illegal Immigration: Border-Crossing Deaths Have Doubled Since 1995; Border Patrol's Efforts to Prevent Deaths
Have Not Been Fully Evaluated," US Government Accountability Office, August 2006, https://www.gao.gov/new.items
/d06770.pdf.

12 John Carlos Frey, "Graves of Shame," *Texas Observer*, July
6, 2015, https://www.texasobserver.org/illegal-mass-graves-of
-migrant-remains-found-in-south-texas/.

13 Interoffice Memorandum, Texas Department of Public
Safety, Texas Rangers, June 6, 2014, https://www.scribd.com
/document/234878018/Texas-Ranger-report#scribd.

14 Mark Collette, "Rangers: No Laws Broken in Border Burials," *Houston Chronicle*, August 17, 2014, http://www.housto
nchronicle.com/news/houston-texas/texas/article/Rangers
-No-laws-broken-in-border-burials-5694604.php.

15 Frey, "Graves of Shame."

16 Frey, "Graves of Shame."

17 Frey, "Graves of Shame."

18 Interoffice Memorandum, Texas Department of Public
Safety, Texas Rangers.

19 Kristian Hernandez, "New Law Addresses Rising Death Toll
of Unidentified Border Crossers," *Brownsville Herald*, June
27, 2015, https://www.brownsvilleherald.com/news/valley/new
-law-addresses-rising-death-toll-of-unidentified-border
-crossers/article_d65da89c-1d41-11e5-8a77-cff837eeeead
.html.

20 Sameen Amin and Lori Jane Gliha, "Making Art from
Migrants' Trash," Al Jazeera America, May 26, 2014, http://
america.aljazeera.com/watch/shows/america-tonight/arti
cles/2014/5/26/undocumented-migrantart.html.

Chapter 6: The Soldiers

1 "Deaths by Border Patrol Since 2010," Southern Border Community Coalition, December 21, 2018, https://www.southernborder.org/deaths_by_border_patrol.

2 John Carlos Frey, "Cruelty on the Border," Salon.com, July 7, 2012, https://www.salon.com/2012/07/20/cruelty_on_the _border/.

3 Trying to get information about incidents through traditional channels like Freedom of Information Act requests or writing or calling CBP officials leads to nothing but dead ends. I have resorted to nurturing contacts within CBP who can provide an insider's view into an opaque agency.

4 John Carlos Frey, Brian Epstein, and Pete Madden, "Life and Death at the Border," *ABC News* 20/20, aired March 6, 2017, https://abcnews.go.com/2020/deepdive/video-border -officers-actions-lead-tragedy-48912222.

5 Frey, Epstein, and Madden, "Life and Death at the Border."

6 This is a pseudonym.

7 "US Border Patrol recruiting Iraq, Afghanistan Veterans," American Legion, December 18, 2018, https://www.legion .org/pressrelease/90330/u-s-border-patrol-recruiting-iraq-af ghanistan-veterans.

8 "Border Patrol Hiring, Training and Infrastructure Issues," National Border Patrol Council, June 2008, http://soboco .org/wp-content/uploads/2013/06/NBPC-report-on-Border -Patrol-Hiring-Training-and-Infrastructure-Issues-June -2008.pdf.

9 James Pinkerton and Susan Carroll, "No Diploma Needed in Border Patrol and Critics Are Worried," *Houston Chronicle*, April 1, 2008, https://www.chron.com/news/nation-world /article/No-diploma-needed-in-Border-Patrol-and-critics -1572429.php.

10 Josiah McC. Heyman, "Why Caution is Needed Before Hiring Additional Border Patrol Agents and ICE Officers,"

American Immigration Council, April 24, 2017, https://www
.americanimmigrationcouncil.org/research/why-caution
-needed-hiring-additional-border-patrol-agents-and-ice
-officers.

11 Pinkerton and Carroll, "No Diploma Needed in Border Patrol."

12 "Border Patrol Hiring," National Border Patrol Council.

13 John Carlos Frey interview with James Tomsheck, August
17, 2017.

14 Sarah Macareg, "Fatal Encounters: 97 Deaths Point to Pattern of Border Agent Violence across America," *Guardian*,
May 2, 2018, https://www.theguardian.com/us-news/2018/may
/02/fatal-encounters-97-deaths-point-to-pattern-of-border
-agent-violence-across-america.

15 "White House Orders the Hiring of 15,000 new Border Agents,"
National Public Radio: Morning Edition, February 22, 2017,
https://www.npr.org/2017/02/22/516582946/white-house
-orders-the-hiring-of-15-000-new-border-agents.

16 "Deaths by Border Patrol Since 2010," Southern Border
Communities Coalition.

17 "A Culture of Cruelty," No More Deaths, February 2011, http://
forms.nomoredeaths.org/wp-content/uploads/2014/10/Cul
tureOfCruelty-full.compressed.pdf.

18 Frey, "Cruelty on the Border."

19 Guillermo Cantor, "Still No Action Taken: Complaints
Against Border Patrol Agents Continue to Go Unanswered,"
American Immigration Council, August 2, 2017, https://
www.americanimmigrationcouncil.org/research/still-no-ac
tion-taken-complaints-against-border-patrol-agents-continue
-go-unanswered.

20 John Carlos Frey and Brian Epstein, "Complaints: Border Officers Engaged in Pattern of 'Egregious' Abuse
against Minors," ABC News, September 14, 2017, https://
abcnews.go.com/US/complaints-border-officers-engaged
-pattern-egregious-abuse-minors/story?id=49845697.

21 Cantor, "Still No Action."

22 John Carlos Frey, "Crossing the Line at the Border," April 20, 2012, Type Investigations, PBS Need to Know, https://typein vestigations.org/project/2013/05/17/death-along-border/.

23 John Carlos Frey, "Over the Line," *Washington Monthly*, June 2013, https://washingtonmonthly.com/magazine/mayjune -2013/over-the-line/.

24 US Customs and Border Protection, *Operational Protocols for Border Violence Incidents*, unpublished document, 2011.

25 "Mexico Condemns Death of Citizen Shot by US Agents," Fox News, June 23, 2011, https://www.foxnews.com/politics /mexico-condemns-death-of-citizen-shot-by-u-s-agents.

26 Richard Marosi, "Human Rights Group Urge Congress to Investigate Border Patrol's Use of Deadly Force," *Los Angeles Times*, June 25, 2011, http://articles.latimes.com/2011/jun /25/local/la-me-border-protest-20110625.

27 Email response by US Customs and Border Protection.

28 John Carlos Frey, "Over the Line."

29 US Customs and Border Protection, *Interim Use of Force and Firearms Guidelines*, unpublished document, n.d.

30 Macareg, "Fatal encounters."

31 Frey and Epstein, "Complaints."

32 Frey and Epstein, "Complaints."

33 Analysis by Type Investigations at the Nation Institute, 2016, https://www.typeinvestigations.org/investigation/2017/09/14 /border-officers-engaged-egregious-abuse/.

34 Frey and Epstein, "Complaints."

Chapter 7: The War at the Border Expands

 1 John Carlos Frey, *The Real Death Valley: Full Length Weather Channel Documentary*, Weather Films, November 11, 2015, https://vimeo.com/109202705.

 2 "Legal Authority for the Border Patrol," US Customs and Border Protection, July 28, 2018, https://help.cbp.gov/app/answers /detail/a_id/1084/~/legal-authority-for-the-border-patrol.

3 "What We Do," US Immigration and Customs Enforcement, December 12, 2018, https://www.ice.gov/overview.

4 "Detention Facilities," US Immigration and Customs Enforcement, February 26, 2019, https://www.ice.gov/detention-facilities.

5 "Legal Authority for the Border Patrol," US Customs and Border Protection.

6 Fernanda Santos, "Border Patrol Accused of Profiling and Abuse," *New York Times*, October 14, 2015, https://www.nytimes.com/2015/10/15/us/aclu-accuses-border-patrol-of-underreporting-civil-rights-complaints.html.

7 "Checkpoints Contribute to Border Patrol's Mission but More Consistent Data Collection and Performance Measurement Could Prove Effectiveness," Government Accountability Office, August 2009, https://www.gao.gov/new.items/d09824.pdf.

8 "The Constitution in the 100 Mile Zone," American Civil Liberties Union, June 21, 2018, https://www.aclu.org/other/constitution-100-mile-border-zone.

9 "Privacy at Borders and Checkpoints," American Civil Liberties Union, accessed February 2019, https://www.aclu.org/issues/privacy-technology/privacy-borders-and-checkpoints.

10 "Legal Noncitizens Receive Longest ICE Detention," TRAC Immigration, June 3, 2013, https://trac.syr.edu/immigration/reports/321/.

11 "Legal Noncitizens Receive Longest Ice Detention," TRAC Immigration.

12 "ICE Detention Facility List," National Immigrant Justice Center, November 2017, https://www.scribd.com/document/373733514/November-2017-ICE-Detention-Facility-Lists#from_embed.

13 "Enacted Border Patrol Program Budget in the United States from 1990–2017 (in million U.S. dollars)," *Statista*, accessed February 26, 2019, https://www.statista.com/statistics/455587/enacted-border-patrol-program-budget-in-the-us/.

14 Geneva Sands, "This Year Saw the Most People in Immigration Detention Since 2001," CNN, November 12, 2018, https://www.cnn.com/2018/11/12/politics/ice-detention/index.html.

15 Amanda Sakuma, "Obama Leaves Behind a Mixed Legacy on Immigration," NBCNews.com, January 15, 2017, https://www.nbcnews.com/storyline/president-obama-the-legacy/obama-leaves-behind-mixed-legacy-immigration-n703656.

16 Muzaffar Chishti, Sarah Pierce, and Jessica Bolter, "The Obama Record on Deportations: Deporter in Chief or Not?" Migration Policy Institute, January 26, 2017, https://www.migrationpolicy.org/article/obama-record-deportations-deporter-chief-or-not.

17 "Lockheed Martin: All Recipients," Opensecrets.org, accessed February 2019, http://www.opensecrets.org/orgs/recips.php?cycle=2012&id=d000000104.

18 "Sen. Charles E. Schumer—New York," Opensecrets.org, accessed February 2019, http://www.opensecrets.org/politicians/contrib.php?cycle=2012&cid=N00001093&type=I.

19 "Sen. Lindsey Graham—South Carolina," Opensecrets.org, accessed February 2019, http://www.opensecrets.org/politicians/contrib.php?cycle=2012&cid=N00009975&type=I.

20 "Sen. Robert Menendez - New Jersey," Opensecrets.org, accessed February 2019, https://www.opensecrets.org/members-of-congress/summary?cid=N00000699&cycle=2012.

21 "Boeing Co: All Recipients," Opensecrets.org, accessed February 2019, http://www.opensecrets.org/orgs/recips.php?cycle=2012&id=D000000100.

22 Gavin Aronsen, "Immigration Reform: Good News for Contractors" *Mother Jones*, June 26, 2013, https://www.motherjones.com/politics/2013/06/immigration-reform-border-security-contractors/.

23 Lee Fang, "Surveillance and Border Security Contractors See Big Money in Donald Trump's Immigration Agenda," *The Intercept*, December 6, 2016, https://theintercept.com/2016/12/06/defense-companies-trump/.

24 Evan Hoopfer, "Lockheed Martin Awarded $22.7 Billion with Most of the Work Coming to Fort Worth," *Dallas Business Journal,* November 14, 2018, https://www.bizjournals .com/dallas/news/2018/11/14/lockheed-martin-awarded-22 -7b-deal-with-most-of.html.

25 Anthony Cappacio, "Lockheed Gets Down Payment for $22 Billion F-35 Buy," Bloomberg, November 14, 2018, https:// www.bloomberg.com/news/articles/2018-11-14/lockheed -gets-down-payment-for-potential-22-billion-f-35-buy.

26 Diedre Walsh and Jeremy Herb, "House Approves Spending Bill With $1.6 Billion for the Border Wall," CNN, July 27, 2017, https://www.cnn.com/2017/07/27/politics/spending-bill -vote-border-wall-money/index.html.

27 John Carlos Frey, "Graves of Shame," *Texas Observer*, July 6, 2015, https://www.texasobserver.org/illegal-mass-graves-of -migrant-remains-found-in-south-texas/.

28 "Border Patrol Search Trauma and Rescue (BORSTAR)," US Customs and Border Protection, February 21, 2019, https://www.cbp.gov/sites/default/files/documents/Border %20Patrol%20Search%2C%20Trauma%2C%20and%20 Rescue.pdf.

29 Analysis of 911 calls performed by Type Investigations.

30 "Immigration Detention 101," Detention Watch Network, February 21, 2019, https://www.detentionwatchnetwork.org /issues/detention-101.

31 Sands, "This Year Saw the Most in Immigration Detention Since 2001."

32 Devlin Barrett, "Private-Prison Firm CCA to Rename Itself CoreCivic," *Wall Street Journal,* October 28, 2016, https:// www.wsj.com/articles/private-prison-firm-cca-to-rename-itself -corecivic-1477666800.

33 "Fiscal Year 2017 ICE Enforcement and Removal Operations Report," US Immigration and Customs Enforcement, October 10, 2018, https://www.ice.gov/sites/default/files/doc uments/Report/2017/iceEndOfYearFY2017.pdf.

34 Andrew Gumbel, "'They Were Laughing at Us': Immigrants Tell of Cruelty, Illness and Filth in US Detention," *Guardian*, September 12, 2018, https://www.theguardian.com/us -news/2018/sep/12/us-immigration-detention-facilities.

35 "How ICE Ignores Death in Detention," National Immigrant Justice Center, February 24, 2016, https://immigrant justice.org/research-items/report-fatal-neglect-how-ice-ignores -deaths-detention?q=fatalneglect.

36 Kate Morrissey, "Report Links Deaths in Immigration Detention to Sub-Par Medical Care," *San Diego Union-Tribune*, June 20, 2018, https://www.sandiegouniontribune.com/news /immigration/sd-me-immigration-deaths-20180620-story.html.

37 John Carlos Frey, Brian Epstein, Tom Llamas, and Pete Madden, "Dying for Salvation," *Nightline*, ABC News, December 13, 2018, https://abcnews.go.com/Nightline/migrant-death -shines-light-allegations-inadequate-medical-care/story?id =59790707.

38 "Code Red," Human Rights Watch, June 20, 2018, https://www .hrw.org/report/2018/06/20/code-red/fatal-consequences -dangerously-substandard-medical-care-immigration#.

39 "Immigration Detention 101," Detention Watch Network.

40 "Code Red," Human Rights Watch.

Chapter 8: Trump

1 "Immigration Court Backlog Tool," TRAC Immigration, November 2018, http://trac.syr.edu/phptools/immigration/court _backlog/.

2 From a Trump rally in Miami on January 16, 2017. https:// www.c-span.org/video/?417864-1/donald-trump-campaigns -miami-florida.

3 "US Refugee Ban: Trump Decried for 'Stomping On' American Values," *Guardian*, January 28, 2017, https://www.the guardian.com/us-news/2017/jan/27/trump-immigration-plan -refugees-vetting-reaction.

4 "State of Washington v. Trump," ACLU, February 2, 2017, https://www.aclu-wa.org/cases/state-washington-v-trump.

5 "Ninth Circuit Court of Appeals No. 17-35105 D.C. No. 2:17-cv-00141," USCourts.gov., February 9, 2017, https://cdn.ca9.uscourts.gov/datastore/opinions/2017/02/09/17-35105.pdf.

6 "Trump, President of the United States v. Hawaii," Supremecourt.gov, April 25, 2018, https://www.supremecourt.gov/opinions/17pdf/17-965_h315.pdf.

7 Liz Robyns and Miriam Jordan, "Apartments Are Stocked, Toys Donated. Only Refugees Are Missing," *New York Times*, May 16, 2018, https://www.nytimes.com/2018/05/16/us/refugee-admissions.html.

8 Guadalupe Gonzales, "You Can't Expedite H-1B Visas Until 2019," *Inc.,* September 19, 2018, https://www.inc.com/guadalupe-gonzalez/uscis-h1b-visa-changes.html.

9 Kimberly Amadeo, "Donald Trump on Immigration, Pros and Cons of His Policies," *The Balance,* January 19, 2019, https://www.thebalance.com/donald-trump-immigration-impact-on-economy-4151107.

10 Amadeo, "Donald Trump on Immigration."

11 Phillip Rucker, "Trump Calls for Office to Support Victims of Crimes by Illegal Immigrants," *Washington Post,* February 28, 2017, https://www.washingtonpost.com/politics/2017/live-updates/trump-white-house/real-time-fact-checking-and-analysis-of-trumps-address-to-congress/trump-calls-for-creation-of-office-to-support-victims-of-crimes-by-illegal-immigrants/?noredirect=on&utm_term=.3e64dc2bfc4c.

12 Amadeo, "Donald Trump on Immigration."

13 Michael D. Shear and Emily Baumgartner, "Trump Administration Aims to Sharply Restrict New Green Cards for Those on Public Aid," *New York Times*, September 22, 2018. https://www.nytimes.com/2018/09/22/us/politics/immigrants-green-card-public-aid.html.

14 Zuzan Cepla, "Fact Sheet: Temporary Protective Status," National Immigration Forum, October 12, 2018, https://

immigrationforum.org/article/fact-sheet-temporary-pro tected-status/; Charles Dunst and Krisnadev Calamur, "Trump Moves to Deport Vietnam War Refugees," *The Atlantic*, December 12, 2018, https://www.theatlantic.com /international/archive/2018/12/donald-trump-deport-vietnam -war-refugees/577993/.

15 Rocio Cara Labrador and Danielle Renwick, "Central America's Violent Northern Triangle," Council on Foreign Relations, June 26, 2018, https://www.cfr.org/backgrounder /central-americas-violent-northern-triangle.

16 "Attorney General Announces Zero-Tolerance for Crimi-nal Illegal Entry," US Department of Justice, April 6, 2018, https://www.justice.gov/opa/pr/attorney-general-announces -zero-tolerance-policy-criminal-illegal-entry.

17 Andrew Cohen, "What 'Taking the Shackles Off' Really Means," Brennan Center for Justice, February 28, 2017, https://www.brennancenter.org/what-taking-the-shackles -off-really-means.

18 "Enforcement Actions at of Focused on Sensitive Locations," US Immigration and Customs Enforcement, memorandum, October 24, 2011, https://www.ice.gov/doclib/ero-outreach /pdf/10029.2-policy.pdf.

19 Andrea Castillo, "Immigrant Arrested by ICE after Drop-ping Daughter Off at School, Sending Shockwaves through Neighborhood," *Los Angeles Times*, March 3, 2017, https:// www.latimes.com/local/lanow/la-me-immigration-school -20170303-story.html.

20 "South LA Mechanic Arrested in Unlawful ICE Raid Caught on Video Won't be Deported," *CBS News Los Angeles*, March 9, 2018, https://losangeles.cbslocal.com/2018/03/09 /aclu-south-la-mechanic-deportation-dismissal/.

21 "How Crossing the US-Mexico Border Became a Crime," *The Conversation*, April 30, 2017, http://theconversation.com /how-crossing-the-us-mexico-border-became-a-crime -74604.

22 Carla Herreria, "565 Migrant Children Remain Separated from Families 3 Weeks Past Judge's Deadline," Huffington Post, August 16, 2018, https://www.huffingtonpost.com/entry /565-migrant-children-still-separated-past-deadline_us _5b7617dee4b018b93e9227ee.

23 John Haltiwanger, "John Kelly Proposed Separating Children from Their Parents to Deter Illegal Immigration Last Year, and Now the Trump Administration Can't Get Its Story Straight," Business Insider, June 18, 2018, https://www.busi nessinsider.com/kelly-proposed-family-separation-to-deter -illegal-immigration-in-2017-2018-6.

24 Manny Fernandez and Katie Benner, "The Billion Dollar Business of Operating Shelters for Migrant Children," New York Times, June 21, 2018, https://www.nytimes.com/2018 /06/21/us/migrant-shelters-border-crossing.html.

25 "Bilingual Youth Care Worker Job," Lensa Job Posting, February 27, 2019, https://lensa.com/bilingual-travel-youth-care -worker-jobs/el-paso/jd/32a688555e44deb254f1f82854c9eac2.

26 Miriam Valverde, "Donald Trump's Executive Order Ending His Administration's Separation of Families," Politifact, June 25, 2018, https://www.politifact.com/truth-o-meter /article/2018/jun/25/donald-trumps-executive-order-ending -his-administr/.

27 Marian Kahn, Geneva Sands, and Trish Turner, "Trump Administration Wants $18B to Build 'Big, Beautiful Wall,'" ABC News, January 5, 2018, https://abcnews.go.com/Pol itics/trump-administration-18b-build-big-beautiful-wall /story?id=52172319.

28 Jordain Carney, "Senate Dems: Trump's Border Wall Could Cost Nearly $70 Billion," The Hill, April 18, 2017, https:// thehill.com/blogs/floor-action/senate/329359-senate-dems -trumps-border-wall-could-cost-nearly-70-billion.

29 Dennis Wagner, "The Wall," USA Today, October 2017, https://www.usatoday.com/border-wall/.

30 Ron Nixon, "Trumps Wall Faces a Barrier in Texas: Landowner Lawsuits," *New York Times*, May 8, 2017, https://www
.news-journal.com/news/nation-world/trump-s-wall-faces
-a-barrier-in-texas-landowner-lawsuits/article_0aa9b419
-a8cd-5ecb-8e20-2041c69b50df.html.

31 Erica Werner and Seung Min Kim, "Trump Backs Off Demand for $5 Billion for Border Wall but Budget Impasse Remains Ahead of Shutdown Deadline," *Washington Post*, December 19, 2018, https://www.washingtonpost.com/business
/economy/white-house-signals-its-backing-down-in-shut
down-dispute-will-find-other-ways-to-fund-border-wall/2018
/12/18/159994dc-02d9-11e9-9122-82e98f91ee6f_story.html?utm
_term=.e17a5e8a5743.

32 Patrick Michels and Andrew Becker, "Contractors Named to Build Border Wall Prototypes," *Reveal*, August 31, 2017, https://www.revealnews.org/blog/cbp-names-4-contractors
-to-build-border-wall-prototypes/.

33 Wagner, "The Wall."

34 Wagner, "The Wall."

35 Andrew Hay, "US Border Deaths Rise on Family, Child Migrants: Patrol Agency," Reuters, June 25, 2018, https://
www.reuters.com/article/us-usa-immigration-deaths/u-s
-border-deaths-rise-on-family-child-migrants-patrol-agency
-idUSKBN1JL33P.

36 "Executive Office for Immigration Review Asylum Rates," US Department of Justice, April 16, 2018, https://www.justice
.gov/eoir/file/1061586/download.

37 Tedd Hesson and Josh Gerstein, "Sessions Moves to Block Asylum for Most Victims, Gang Violence," *Politico*, June 11, 2018, https://www.politico.com/story/2018/06/11/jeff-sessions
-aslyum-standards-domestic-violence-614158.

38 "Asylum Decisions and Denials Jump in 2018," TRAC Immigration, November 29, 2018, https://trac.syr.edu/immi
gration/reports/539/.

39 Alan Gomez, Hasan Dudar, and Bill Theobald, "Caravan of Exaggeration," *USA Today*, October 23, 2018, https://www .usatoday.com/story/news/politics/2018/10/23/migrant-car avan-president-trump-claims-includes-middle-easterners /1742685002/.

40 "New Study Examines Links Between Emigration and Food Insecurity in the Dry Corridor of El Salvador, Guatemala and Honduras," World Food Programme, August 23, 2017, https://www.wfp.org/news/news-release/new-study-examines -links-between-emigration-and-food-insecurity-dry-corridor -el-sa.

41 Anastasia Moloney, "Two Million Risk Hunger After Drought in Central America," Reuters, September 7, 2018, https://www.reuters.com/article/us-americas-drought-un /two-million-risk-hunger-after-drought-in-central-america -un-idUSKCN1LN2AY.

42 "Food Security and Emigration," World Food Programme, August 2017, https://docs.wfp.org/api/documents/WFP-000 0022124/download/?_ga=2.111856772.1483336788 .1550775024-1324541223.1547058131.

Conclusion

1 "US Border Patrol Southwest Border Apprehensions by Sector FY 2018," Customs and Border Protection, October 23, 2018, https://www.cbp.gov/newsroom/stats/usbp-sw -border-apprehensions.

2 Cristianna Silva, "15 Martin Luther Jr., Quotes That Still Resonate in Today's America," *Newsweek*, January 15, 2018, https://www.newsweek.com/martin-luther-king-jr-quotes -still-resonate-todays-america-780643.

Index

Credit: Aaron Jay Young

John Carlos Frey is an investigative reporter and documentary filmmaker based in Los Angeles. A five-time Emmy Award winner, he is a special correspondent for *PBS NewsHour* and a longtime Type Investigations journalist. His work has also been reported on *60 Minutes*, ABC News, CBS News, NBC News, *Dan Rather Reports*, PBS NewsHour, the Huffington Post, Salon.com, the *Los Angeles Times*, *Washington Monthly*, and *El Diario*. His documentary films include *America Burning*, *The Source*, *The Hunger That Consumes You*, *Cruel and Unusual?*, *Exodus*, *Hidden Cost*, and *The Real Death Valley*. He is a recipient of the Scripps Howard Award, the Sigma Delta Chi award, the IRE Medal, and the Polk Award, among others, for his investigative work.